THE MASTER BOOK OF SPIES

WRITTEN AND ADVISED BY
Donald McCormick

The Master Book of Spies

the world of espionage
master spies, tortures, interrogations
spy equipment, escapes, codes
& how you can become a spy

Franklin Watts, Inc. · New York, N.Y.
1976

First published in 1973 in Great Britain
by Hodder Causton Ltd.

First American publication 1974
Second impression 1976
by Franklin Watts, Inc.

Copyright © 1973 by Hodder Causton Ltd.
Copyright © 1974 by Hodder Causton Ltd.
SBN: 531- 02415-6.
Library of Congress Catalog Card Number: 73-11897
Printed in Great Britain
by Sir Joseph Causton & Sons Ltd

The Russians are much more thorough in arranging contacts with new agents. Perhaps they go to ridiculous lengths, but one point they wish to establish at the beginning with a new agent is that his memory is faultless, as well as ensuring that a code phrase is not so simple that it can be answered correctly, if unknowingly, by someone who is not the required agent.

The best example of the Russian method of contact is that supplied by Alexander Foote, an Englishman who was recruited by the Soviet Secret Service shortly before World War II. Foote, in his book *Handbook for Spies*, tells how he was instructed in London that he was 'to present myself outside the General Post Office in Geneva (a favourite rendezvous, as a GPO is easily found and provides an admirable excuse for loitering). I was to be wearing a white scarf and to be holding in my right hand a leather belt. As the clock struck noon I would be approached by a woman carrying a string shopping bag containing a green parcel; she would also be holding an orange in her hand. One would have thought that this would have been sufficient to enable anyone to contact anyone, even an unknown, in the middle of a Swiss street. But to avoid any possibility of error the whole rendezvous was made even more precise. The woman would ask me, in English, where I had bought the belt, and I was to reply that I had bought it in an ironmonger's shop in Paris. Then I was to ask her if I could buy an orange like hers, and she was to say that I could have hers for an English penny. Hardly sparkling dialogue, but sufficient to ensure that the meeting was foolproof and an example of the usual thoroughness of my employers...'

'Toni's' rendezvous at the British Museum led him by way of taxi to a London restaurant and from there to a 'recruitment office ... I was never allowed out of sight of my contact for a moment. I was even accompanied to the lavatory'.

He was asked if he would serve the American cause and then given an intensive cross-examination. By this time they had checked up on the family in Hong Kong with whom he had stayed and satisfied themselves that they were anti-Communist, but they still required to fill in details of 'Toni's' career, even down to a report from his prep school headmaster.

This is fairly typical of a certain type of recruitment adopted by most of the world's espionage services. Of course, in a career where individualism counts for as much as discipline, methods of recruitment must vary not only as regards one country and another, but one individual and another. In the case of 'Toni' the spy-masters were looking for someone who would be loyal, who had a fluency in Chinese and Japanese and who was a man of the world who had travelled around.

started to check on his background. The information was
encouraging and they decided that 'Toni' might well be the
kind of recruit they were looking for.

Inquiries were made in the vicinity of the English village
in which he was living. What worried the Americans, however,
was that he had spent some time in Hong Kong with a Chinese
family. Two possibilities presented themselves: first, that
'Toni' might already be working for British Intelligence,
second, that he might even be a secret sympathiser of Mao
Tse-tung. At this time the United States Intelligence was
extremely suspicious of anyone who had links with the
Chinese, even if they were living outside China. It was the
era of national witch-hunting against suspected Communists.

Hence the contrived casual meeting with 'Toni' in a
country pub by the American stranger. It was not too difficult
to bring the subject round to that of radio 'hams' and soon the
stranger was invited round to 'Toni's' house to see his
transmitter set and equipment.

What sort of a job was 'Toni' looking for? 'Well', replied
the radio 'ham', 'something with a touch of adventure.'
Curious though it may seem, the one thing that worried the
US Intelligence officer was this confession. Espionage may
lead to adventure, but for most of the time it is slow, plodding,
unadventurous work that only occasionally provides an
element of thrills. This is certainly the case if the agent wants
to last the course.

So the crucial question put to 'Toni' was 'If you really
want adventure, why not become a mercenary soldier?' This
was, of course, casually put, after leading up gradually to the
subject of excitement in life. Luckily for him, 'Toni' gave
the right reply: 'A mercenary's life is not adventure as I see
it. I want the kind of adventure to which I can apply my
talents and those are not a mercenary's talents.'

This was the answer the stranger wanted to hear, so he
gave 'Toni' a hint that, if he was interested, there might
well be scope for his talents. Would he go to the British
Museum on such and such a day and a certain time, make
an application for a certain book that would be given to
him at a seat in the North Gallery and there he would be
contacted.

He was told that he would be approached by another
stranger who would say to him: 'I think you know Ernest
Hemingway's wife.' The reply he was to give was: 'No, but
I knew her former husband.'

Contact was duly established in this manner. It was simple,
but by some standards it could have been too simple, even
disastrously simple. As 'Toni' told me long afterwards 'a
score of people might have known her former husband in
various parts of the world. After all he was a much travelled
war correspondent, known to many'.

Contents

Foreword

This is an attempt at the whole inside story of spying, not merely its history, or how each nation tackles it, but those normally avoided questions of how one becomes a spy, what spying is like and how it all works.

It is an awful lot to say in relatively few words and at the same time to try to answer all the questions that readers will want to know. Not least will they want to know why I, personally, claim to know the answers.

I could simply say that it has been a life-time's hobby. If one collected stamps, or coins, that would satisfy most. But to anticipate your queries, I can also say that I have known many spies and some of them have been my friends. Some, too, have been my enemies. But I have always tried to judge both friends and enemies according to their merits: one can learn much from each.

Have I myself spied? Well, there are some limits to what one can confess. But can I just say this—and it should encourage all potential spies, because this is a task well within their scope, if they are patient and conscientious—in 1942 I made a totally unauthorised entry into the out-of-bounds Kasbah of Algiers to work out a detailed street map of this still enemy-infested territory.

For whom? None other than Ian Fleming, creator of James Bond, and at that time Deputy Director of British Naval Intelligence.

Donald McCormick

Chapter 1

How to be a spy

'Toni' was recruited into the spy game after a casual encounter with a stranger in a country club.

'Toni' was his code-name. It is one quite often chosen for spies, partly because it is common and unlikely to attract undue attention, but mainly because it sounds very much the same however it is pronounced in any language. Many a serious slip-up can occur if a spy has a code-name which can, by being mispronounced, be taken for something else.

Now the stranger knew quite a lot already about 'Toni'. He had learned that 'Toni' was an enthusiastic radio 'ham', that his father had been British and his mother American, that both his parents were dead and he was unmarried. 'Toni' had been educated in Switzerland, a country he knew well, and at Cambridge where he had taken a degree in oriental languages. He spoke French, Chinese and Japanese fluently. These qualifications alone were sufficient for him to be considered as a potential recruit to the world of espionage without his taking any steps to offer his services. But the recruiters still required to know much more about him. The fact is that if 'Toni' had had fewer qualifications, and if the powers-that-be had known his background in greater detail and if his family had all served in Intelligence before him, it would probably have been much easier for him to be accepted.

'Toni' had only come down from Cambridge a few months previously and had spent a month practising his languages with a Chinese family in Hong Kong. He had returned to his home in the south-east of England to write a thesis for his MA degree. During this time he had constructed his own radio transmitter, aiming to establish a two-way radio communications system that would be simple to operate.

He established contact with other 'hams' in various parts of the world. Sometimes he picked up broadcasts in English

**An example of
ham radio equipment**

put out by Arab guerrillas, at other times he intercepted foreign police messages in international code. Then one day he had a communication from North Korea asking if he would monitor their test transmissions. The fact that he had established this communications link was reported in his local paper.

An American saw the brief report and interview with 'Toni' and sent it to the American Intelligence. Shortly afterwards 'Toni' had a letter from an American asking him if he could pass a message to his son who was a prisoner-of-war in North Korea. 'Toni' sent a radio message to the North Koreans and they told him to pass any such messages or letters via a post box number in Poland.

It was this incident that drew the attention of the United States Intelligence to 'Toni'. They were impressed by the fact that he had made no attempt to keep this secret, but had reported the matter to the local newspaper. Immediately they

**The local newspaper's report
on 'Toni's' contact with
North Korea**

The small back room of his ▮▮▮▮▮▮▮ house in ▮▮▮▮▮ must now be one of the most sophisticated—if unlikely — private monitoring stations in the w o r l d. Here amid the Regency striped wallpaper and a clutter of souvenirs ▮▮▮ does his global eavesdropping.

He said: "I had an aproach from the Liberation Radio Station ▮ ▮▮▮▮▮ asking if I would monitor their test trans-missions. They had taken my name from a directory listing people with suitable equipment.

"I began a regular contact with them and sometimes they would send me propaganda pictures of the damage the American bombs were causing.

"Then o n e d a y an American friend was here, heard about my ▮▮▮▮▮ link, and asked if I could try to get a message through to his nephew who was a prisoner-of-war there."

But it was his knowledge of radio transmission that really clinched this job.

There is no single way to be a spy. It all depends upon what the would-be recruit has to offer. Recruitment is generally governed by which type of spy is needed at a given moment.

Usually it is a case of the seekers for spies taking the initiative rather than the would-be spy asking to be recruited. Spy-masters prefer to make their own assessments first, to spot a likely recruit and to screen him thoroughly before making an approach. It is much more difficult for the would-be spy to get himself accepted on his own approaches.

If you want to be a spy you must either be a person of unswerving and proved loyalty to the country you wish to serve, or somebody who has certain talents and know-how that another country needs at all costs. Paradoxically, it should be stressed that loyalty alone is not enough, and secondly it is possible, even if you are suspected of being a man of divided loyalties, that the information to which you have access may outweigh other objections. The British tended over the centuries to put a premium on loyalty and 'a sound family background'. This paid off very well until a few devious individuals managed to pose as loyal subjects and, because of their unimpeachable backgrounds, to be accepted as such. The most blatant and impudent exploitation of this dependence on family background was that of 'Kim' Philby, son of a distinguished British knight, who, already recruited into the Soviet Intelligence in 1933, wrote that while working for *The Times* as a war correspondent in the early summer of 1940, he 'watched the various irons I had put in the fire, nudging one or other of them as they appeared to hot up'. He had a telephone call from the Foreign Editor of *The Times*, asking if he was 'available for war work' and, in his own words, 'soon afterwards I found myself in the forecourt

Harold 'Kim' Philby. British Traitor, defected 1963, giving a press conference

'Kim' Philby, son of Harry St John Bridger Philby, officer of the Indian Civil Service, during the Spanish Civil War

of the St Ermin's Hotel, near St James's Park Station, talking to ... an intensely likeable elderly lady ... She spoke with authority and was evidently in a position to recommend me for "interesting" employment ... I passed the examination'.

But it is unlikely that anyone of 'sound family background' could today become an Intelligence agent quite so easily.

On the other hand the Russians, when employing foreigners, have tended to play on disloyalty and have suffered from loyalists posing as being traitors.

Thus the two basic and to some extent opposed qualifications for being a spy are unquestioned loyalty and the possession of something worth passing on. While the person in the latter category can take care of himself, what else does the former require in the way of qualifications?

Fluency in a number of languages will obviously help, though many spies have done without it. This enables an agent to operate in different countries. Specialised scientific knowledge can also be an asset, especially in the field of electronics or nuclear science and modern weaponry. If a man can assess accurately and interpret clearly what he sees or knows, whether it is some complicated piece of new machinery or the lay-out of an arms factory, so much the better.

An acquaintance with radio techniques such as 'Toni' had and the ability to use a radio transmitter set will again be an asset. A detailed knowledge of certain countries can be useful, particularly of the lesser-known countries, and the facility for making frequent visits to a country for which visas are not normally easily obtainable can again be helpful.

If you are academically-minded and have a gift for code-breaking, this may be regarded as invaluable, though it will probably mean you are no better than a back-room spy. Many university men have been recruited into espionage because of a certain mathematical turn of mind and a talent for deciphering and analysing coded messages.

The above qualifications will obviously commend themselves to any spy-master, or recruiter. But there are many lesser qualifications which will fit the bill. A gregarious man who knows a great number of people in all walks of life, who is kept well-informed about new developments in the area in which he lives, may, without knowing it, be just the kind of person the Intelligence Services are looking for. They want to be able to turn to somebody at a moment's notice and say: 'What do you know about so-and-so?' or 'can you tell us why "X" is spending so much time at "Z"?'

A perfect spy may be a person totally without technical qualifications yet in a position to pass on vital information. He might be a bartender at a sea-port, or a man delivering goods at a military air base, or even a street newspaper seller whose stand is close to a foreign embassy and who can observe people going in and out of that building.

A newspaperman near a foreign embassy. An ideal look-out post and cover for a spy

'Toni' was spotted first and recruited without expecting it. How about the man who wants to be a spy and doesn't know how to set about it? His task is much more difficult because he has to sell himself and anybody who seeks a job as a spy is at first naturally suspect. Indeed one of the jobs given to experienced spies is to check up on would-be spies.

The potential recruit will need to be able to eliminate all possible causes for suspicion and to prove that he has something to offer. In the first place he must be able to supply a complete dossier on his early life from birth onwards. If there are any gaps in the narrative, even of a few months, the authorities are at once on the alert as to whether they are being infiltrated by an enemy agent.

Some espionage services take on recruits and give them a completely new identity. Sometimes, though rarely, this is done at an exceptionally early age. For example, Konon Trofimovich Molody, a Russian, was, at the age of eleven, taken to the United States, bearing a Canadian passport in the name of Gordon Arnold Lonsdale, by an aunt who passed herself off as his mother. The real Lonsdale had been born at Cobalt, Ontario, in 1924, so his age matched that of Molody to within a year. The original Lonsdale had been taken to Finland by his mother in 1932 and nothing had been heard of him since. This was one of the Russians' first experiments in long-term espionage and Molody became one of their ace agents. Much later, as will be seen, he was to become organiser of a major spy-ring inside Britain.

Thus today all espionage services tend to be on their guard against infiltration and a very thorough check is made on the careers of would-be agents. The career dossier provided by the recruit is carefully checked against independent reports. The Americans, who have learned their lessons well in this respect, often want to know the details of a recruit right from the days of his first school, even to the extent of examining school reports for any signs of behaviour patterns.

Assuming that the would-be spy can provide a satisfactory dossier on his career to date and that this has been checked and found correct, the next step is an analysis of his personality. In some cases he may be checked by a psychiatrist. It is important to learn whether he has any phobias or personality quirks which would jeopardise his work as an agent. A dread of being in confined spaces would probably rule him out and so, too, would be a tendency to talk indiscreetly after a few drinks.

The next question would be what he had to offer the country he wished to serve. If, for example, he could claim he had a knowledge of an underground network of saboteurs and anarchists at his college or university, this might be listened to with interest. Or if he was going on holiday to a certain country where he would be staying with someone who

Konon Trofimovish Molody, alias Gordon Arnold Lonsdale. He was sentenced to 25 years for espionage in Great Britain, but three years later, he was exchanged for British business man Greville Wynne

knew about certain subversive activities, this alone might arouse interest. Subject to certain safeguards, he might be asked to prove himself on a minor assignment.

After that it is up to the would-be spy to prove his own value. It will inevitably take longer for the would-be spy to be accepted than for the individual who is sought out by the Intelligence Services. But once he has proved himself over a lengthy period, he will probably be accepted. All this may seem frustrating, but he must realise that if spy-masters are not suspicious of would-be recruits, they are not efficient. To be too quickly accepted should suggest to the would-be recruit a lack of normal precautions on the part of the recruiters.

How does one set about becoming a spy? There is no single rule for the simple reason that Intelligence Services, being by reason of their business secret, do not advertise for spies, nor do they normally reveal where their offices are, nor the names of their leading personnel. It depends entirely on circumstances. If you have a relative who has been connected with an Intelligence Service, this is probably the easiest way of getting an introduction to a recruiter.

If not, then you must try to find some friend who will give you the name of somebody who knows somebody else in an Intelligence Service. You could, of course, just make contact with some section of a Government Ministry concerned with one or other of the branches of Intelligence, but, unless you had something very positive to offer, this could be a very unrewarding approach. Alternatively, if you are very dedicated to the idea of spying, and are prepared to wait a long time, you could join one of the military or naval services and express a preference for work in, say, the Intelligence Corps.

Ievno Aseff:
The Russian Judas

One of the ablest, if most sinister, spies in history managed to get himself accepted with the minimum of qualifications. His name was Ievno Azeff, the son of a poor Jewish tailor, and it is highly doubtful if today he would be selected by any espionage service. Nevertheless, rogue as Azeff was, his pertinacity in seeking employment as a spy, despite the odds being loaded against him, should serve as a model to encourage others.

By the year 1892 Ievno Azeff had been a clerk, a tutor, a commercial traveller and a reporter on a local Russian newspaper. He had been suspected of having distributed revolutionary propaganda and had married a young revolutionary. His arrest seemed imminent, especially as he had just absconded with the money he had obtained from selling a consignment of butter.

He disappeared into Germany where he entered a Polytechnic Institute. Then, on 4 April, 1893, Ievno decided that the way to safety and to money was to betray his friends in a Russian Social Democratic Group that had been established in Karlsruhe. He wrote to the Russian Police Department, setting out the aims of the group and giving a list of their names, asking for a reply to be sent to a certain address, but omitting his true name.

The following month Ievno received this cagey reply:

We know of the Karlsruhe Group and we are not very interested in it; therefore you are not of such great value to us; nevertheless, we are prepared to pay you on condition, however, that you reveal your name, for we have strict principles and will have no dealings with certain people.

Уже пришла к нашему сведению эта группа в Карлсруэ, но мы ей не особенно интересуемся: следовательно, вы нам не так полезны. Мы все-таки готовы заплатить за сведения, только на условии, что вы откроете нам свою фамилию, так как мы имеем строгие принципы, и не хотим вести дела с некоторыми определенными лицами.

The letter from the Russian Police Department to Aseff.

In fact the *Ochrana*, who were then the key organisation in Russian Intelligence, knew nothing whatsoever about the Karlsruhe Group and were extremely interested in them. So Ievno had stumbled across the right kind of information at the very moment when it was most needed. This is the supreme qualification for the would-be spy.

He replied at once and asked for only fifty roubles a month in pay, but did not reveal his name, thus taking a risk by disobeying instructions. The *Ochrana* were by no means lax and they established his identity by his handwriting and discovered that he must have gone to Karlsruhe from Rostov. There is little doubt that they realised they were dealing with a fugitive from justice. But they were impressed by his contacts with student revolutionaries and took him on as an agent. By 1899 his salary was raised to 100 roubles a month and, as a result of his steady flow of reports on revolutionaries abroad, this steadily increased until he more than doubled his pay. By the early 1900's he was getting 500 roubles a month, an incredibly large sum for an *Ochrana* agent in those days.

We shall learn more of Ievno Azeff's activities in another chapter.

One word of warning on how not to become a spy. Brash young men – and women, too – living abroad have been known to call on their Embassy or Consulate to offer their services as spies. This is guaranteed to get them the swift brush-off. It is a tradition, indeed an unwritten rule, in most Western diplomatic services that diplomats do not dabble in espionage. A cynic may reply that nevertheless some of them do so. But even if this is the case (and it is the rare exception rather than the rule), they dare not admit it for the simple reason that if diplomats are discovered to be mixed up in espionage, they are usually ordered to leave the country. A diplomatic scandal is then publicly blazoned in the press and it may take months, if not years, before normal relations are restored.

If you must seek out someone connected with an Embassy, the best plan is to try to meet one of its Army, Navy or Air Force attachés outside the precincts of the Embassy or Consulate. There is a good reason for this : in some countries local spies keep a close watch on who goes in and out of embassies.

Yet even the Service attaché is likely to give you short shrift unless you have something worthwhile offering in the way of information.

Most of the great powers have a resident local head of Secret Service in all the chief capitals. He is for obvious reasons quite unconnected with his Embassy or Consulate and

may be a man living quietly in retirement, or a well-known
local business man. If you can find out who he is, which,
curiously enough, is not always as difficult as it may seem, he
could be able to help you.

However, for anyone contemplating such a course of action,
it is advisable, if you are living in a foreign country, to
register with your Consulate on arrival, giving your name and
address, and to re-register each year. By this means you
establish your credentials to some extent and when a check is
made on you, it will be easier for the authorities to make an
assessment. Whatever you do, don't go around asking people
who your local head of Secret Service is!

There is one unorthodox and highly dangerous method of
getting recruited as a spy for your country and this is to
penetrate the ranks of a potential enemy nation. It is not one
to be recommended, as infiltration generally requires a
knowledge of intelligence techniques and the espionage game
which a would-be spy could not possibly possess. But, on
occasions, it has been successfully done.

A young American soldier serving in Germany was so
desperately keen to enter the spy game that he deliberately
deserted from the US Forces and slipped across into East
Berlin. Before doing so, however, he left a letter at an
American Consulate stating what he intended to do and
explaining that his purpose was to infiltrate the Intelligence
Service of the Soviet Union. Once he had accomplished this
mission, he stated, he would send a postcard to a certain
address in Germany saying 'Please give Diane and Hazel my
love'.

It was a madcap adventure to attempt for he risked arrest
at the hands of the Russians as a spy and a court martial from
the Americans for desertion. Worse than this he ran the danger
of being forced to work for the Soviet on penalty of death.

But Jack Calloway – that is not his real name – managed to
persuade the Russians that he was deserting from the US
Forces because he hated the 'Cold War' and had come to see
the Soviet point of view. Naturally he was treated with
considerable suspicion, but nevertheless given asylum and
sent to East Germany.

If he wanted to serve the Soviet Union, what information
could he give, inquired the KGB officers who interrogated him.
He gave them a certain amount of innocuous detail about the
US Forces in West Germany, not enough to impress the
KGB, but certainly enough to warrant a charge by the US
authorities. Then he was given a thorough examination into
his whole career to date. He was required to set down on
paper in the greatest detail all the addresses at which he had
lived and the names and addresses of all his relatives.

Jack Calloway had taken the precaution of stating in his
letter to the US authorities every detail which he proposed to

pass on to the Soviet authorities. This included information about an operational code which was not top secret and one that could easily be changed at short notice without much difficulty. To impress the Soviet authorities he had memorised the code and had not written it down. The ability to memorise invariably impresses Intelligence men. But for this it is quite possible that he would have been refused asylum and merely sent back to await court martial...

For two months he was kept in semi-captivity, quite well treated but always under scrutiny. In that period he managed to improve his knowledge of Russian. In due course he was accepted as an agent and given several minor assignments. Eighteen months later he was actually allowed out of East Germany and sent on a mission to Finland. Once there he sent off the postcard with the code message to Diane and Hazel.

**The postcard from Finland:
everything had gone
according to plan**

**Interrogation of 'Jack
Calloway' by the KGB**

Not long afterwards the CIA (Central Intelligence Agency of the United States) contacted him in Helsinki. From that moment he became a double-agent, genuinely serving the USA, but still pretending to act for the Soviet Union.

But, as I have said, this is not a method of self-recruitment to be adopted as a general rule. It is far too dangerous and it is only possible to tell the story today because Jack Calloway is no longer a double-agent.

'Toni's' introduction to the twilight world of spies was extremely thorough. He was made welcome, put at his ease, wined and dined and then put through a series of interviews with relentless cross-examination.

'They went through my whole life over and over again, asking the same question again two days later, just to see if I gave a different answer, I suppose. I can see their point. To some extent I was a foreigner to them. My father was British

Donald Maclean. He was head of the American Department of the Foreign Office, before he disappeared while under suspicion of being a Russian spy in 1951

and I had not been educated in America. And at that time they were very, very suspicious of educated Britons. They saw a Maclean or Philby behind every public schoolboy face'.

'Toni' was given medical examinations and grilled by a psychiatrist. 'The trick cyclist', said 'Toni', using typically English slang for a profession which is rather more revered in the United States than in Britain, 'wanted to find out if I had a mother or a father fixation. I think he worked on the basis that if I had a yen for my father, I would be pro-British, and if I doted on my mother, I would be pro-American. It wasn't like that at all. I just happened to like both countries almost equally. I think that put him out of his stride: it didn't fit the text-book.

'But, joking apart, one must remember that the spy-masters have to be pretty sure of their spies. They must be doubly sure when a spy has parents of different races'.

'Toni' did admit that in the very early stages he was tempted once or twice to call the whole thing off. 'Then I began to realise that all they were doing was to test me out and that they would hardly go to all this trouble unless they had in mind rather important work for me to do. With a lesser agent they wouldn't attempt to flatter his ego so much'.

After that 'Toni' was handed on to the technicians. They made a thorough examination of his radio equipment, asked for all his notes on the monitoring of messages and broadcasts. He was questioned about his radio contacts with North Korea and several somewhat cryptic conversations with other radio 'hams'.

Then they got down to details of his probable future work. 'You will need to be able to set up your own radio equipment from scratch in some circumstances', they said. 'You may have to abandon and destroy your own set to avoid discovery. It is essential that you should, with not too much difficulty, be able to assemble a set again without any aid from outside'.

'Toni' pointed out that a new receiving and transmitting set could be constructed fairly quickly from parts salvaged from a radio receiver and using only basic tools. Much later he did have to abandon sets and start building again. 'It was obvious that the transmitter would have to be something of a compromise, because if I used the valves from a radio receiver, they were not really intended for this type of work. I conducted some experiments and found that most of the recent audio output pentodue and beam tetrode valves would operate in a satisfactory manner.

'I decided to make the transmitter crystal-controlled as this required fewer components, was much easier to build and did not require a mass of test instruments to set up, and, above all, the crystal frequency was very accurate even with quite large variations in mains voltage.

'Crystals for this kind of application are available in a wide variety of mounts – some no larger than a postage stamp, and

Donald Maclean and 'Kim' Philby were members of highly respectable British families who deserted to the Soviet cause.

Part of the basic equipment that a spy might be forced to use. A multimeter

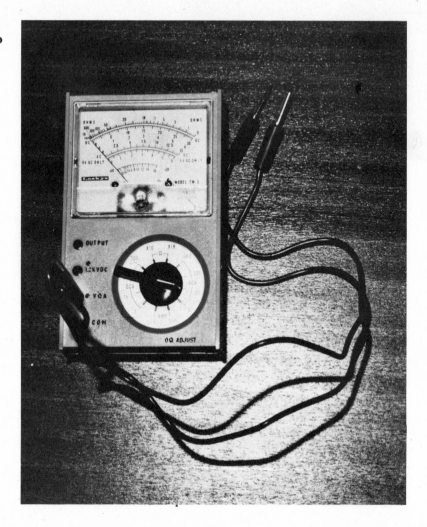

about one millimetre thick, which was important as it meant that a resourceful spy would not have much trouble in hiding them.

'As for the multi-meter, if a spy was driving his own car, he might have one of the dash instruments convertible to a multi-meter, or if he was travelling by other means a photographic light-meter could well be a disguised multi-meter'.

When 'Toni' was forced to build a new set from scratch after his original apparatus had been destroyed it took him four hours to build the circuit and, he told me, 'it would not take anyone else more than six to seven hours to build even if he had never attempted to build such an instrument before'.

Listening to 'Toni' should fill any would-be spy with confidence. He has had to abandon his radio equipment on two occasions, luckily each time he was able to destroy it completely. But his improvised transmitting set enabled him to maintain a reliable contact of up to 250-300 miles and during peak propagation periods from 1,000-2,000 miles.

Chapter 2

They walk alone

Strictly speaking, the word spy only covers the agent of an Intelligence Service who is used only for spying, or, as they call it in the jargon of the British Secret Service, works for the 'old firm'.

But the actual career of a spy may lead him into all the by-paths of espionage with an enormous variety of jobs. Some Intelligence Services – the British, for example – keep the work of spies and spy-catchers in separate departments which work quite independently from one another. But in many other Services the spy of today may become the spy-catcher of tomorrow, or vice versa.

The spy very often shows a bantering contempt for the spy-catcher, regarding him as little more than a policeman. This is, however, unfair: the spy-catcher is frequently engaged in exacting and exciting work, sometimes involving some danger. His job is to sift reports on suspected spies said to be operating in his country, to track them down and, only when he has amassed all the evidence and successfully trapped them, to hand over the job of arrest to the police.

This at least is how it works in most Western countries. Apart from being the fairest method in a democracy – it puts the job of proving espionage on the spy-catchers and ensures a trial in a civil court – it is also the most practical in that it keeps the spy-catchers out of the limelight. A photograph of police arresting a suspected spy would not matter if it appeared in a newspaper. A picture of a spy-catcher doing the same thing would be tantamount to revealing his identity to the enemy.

In Britain it is the task of MI5 to keep tabs on suspected spies, but they have no powers of arrest. The Special Branch (Police) of Scotland Yard are called in to detain and charge the culprits. But in totalitarian countries arrests are usually made by the Secret Police, or spy-catchers, and a suspect may in

A spy being taken to his trial.
Alexandre Sokolov

consequence be detained and imprisoned for months, even years, without being charged or brought to trial. Not infrequently the object of this is to force a confession by threatening to bring a charge.

Espionage, like business, requires its executives and administrators. It follows that the whole existence of the spy must depend on the key men who sit at desks in hush-hush offices examining reports from agents, sending out orders, controlling movements and postings of spies and conducting investigations. The back-room boys may be promoted spies who have proved their ability to be capable of administrative work. More often, however, they have never been 'in the field' (as the work of a spy overseas is described) and remain back-room boys throughout their careers in Intelligence. Such executives are drawn from retired officers in the Armed Forces, the Civil Service and occasionally from business and

Faceless Executives of the Spy Game. Spy chiefs from the film the Ipcress File

banking and the ranks of university professors.

These executives are really the policy-makers of the Secret Services. They maintain liaison with their Foreign Offices and Ministries of Defence; it is their job to see that Secret Service activities do not run counter to foreign policy, or that, if they do, they are not found out. It may seem odd that they should wish occasionally to carry out some activity that is against Government policy, but this happens not infrequently.

Perhaps the biggest scandal of this kind in recent times was the 'Spy in the Sky' affair of Gary Powers, the U-2 pilot who was shot down over the Soviet frontier. In April, 1960, the statesmen of the Western World were trying to bring an end to the state of 'cold war' between the Soviet Union and the West and to have top-level talks with their 'enemies'. The foreign policy of the Western powers at that time was not to provoke Russia in any way.

Francis Gary Powers. The 'Spy in the Sky' shot down over Russia on May Day 1960

But American Intelligence desperately needed to know in an age of thermo-nuclear weapons what death-dealing installations were being set up behind the Iron Curtain. The best and quickest way of learning this was by using the 500 m.p.h., high altitude flying U-2 to obtain photographic evidence. It was the perfect plane for observing missiles, pin-pointing missile bases and checking radiation fall-out. At a great height it was virtually out of reach of fighter planes and missiles.

Gary Powers was assigned for special duties by the CIA. After intensive training he was sent to the Incirlik military air base in Turkey to form part of the Reconnaissance Detachment which was supposed to be carrying out meteorological tests. In fact he made a number of flying missions along the Russian frontiers and sometimes deep inside them.

Then on 1 May, 1960, Gary Powers set out on his last secret flight. He soared into Soviet territory and began working his costly automatic infra-red cameras. What happened on that mission is still somewhat of a mystery. Powers reported that his engine flamed out and that he dived to 40,000 feet, hoping he could start it up again. The Russians claimed that one of their rockets hit the plane at 68,000 feet.

Powers parachuted to the ground inside Soviet territory and was swiftly arrested. The Russians immediately launched a propaganda campaign, indignantly protesting that at the very moment they were about to have a summit conference with the Western Powers, the United States was conducting 'aggressive espionage' inside their territory.

This caused considerable embarrassment in the US State Department who issued a denial that the U-2 had deliberately violated Russian air space and officials put out reports that the plane was engaged on meteorological tests. Unfortunately when Powers was arrested the Russians had found that, apart from emergency food supplies, he had with him a flashlight,

The wreckage of the U-2, the spy plane that Powers was flying

compasses, money in Russian, Italian and German currencies, a dagger, a pistol, gold coins and a silver dollar fitted with a needle containing a lethal dose of the poison curare.

It is, of course, traditional for Governments to deny all knowledge of spies who are caught and to profess ignorance of what has been going on. Nobody believes such protestations, but, to prevent such incidents being escalated into dangerous situations which could bring two nations to the point of war, there are sound diplomatic reasons for such prevarication. It is then that Governments put pressure on the Secret Service departments to reduce or cancel their activities in a certain area for the time being.

But on this occasion the United States Government eventually broke with tradition. On May 7, 1960, on the instructions of President Eisenhower, the State Department admitted that flights over Soviet territory had taken place 'without official authorisation'. Finally Eisenhower himself took full responsibility for having authorised the intelligence flights. This was one of the very few occasions on which the unwritten law of spying was broken by a Governmental admission of complicity.

There are as many different types of spy as there are of an actor. Perhaps there is a parallel in that all spies have to be actors to some extent. There is the radio operator spy whose job is solely to send and receive messages, to keep his equipment in working order and to see that it is destroyed when discovery seems imminent.

Quite important, too, is the paymaster-spy whose duty it is not only to see that agents get their salaries and expenses paid regularly, but to arrange for this to be done without drawing any attention to the source of the money. For this reason it may be necessary for a spy based in, say, Belgrade to go to Switzerland to draw his pay.

Switzerland's laws protect the clients of banks, allowing them to have numbered accounts, the details of which must not be revealed on pain of severe penalties. These laws have been amended in recent years so that criminals can be tracked down, but they still protect the spy and the tax-dodger. In World War II one of the chief pay-centres for spies was the free money market of the then International Zone of Tangier. A spy in Tangier could easily and unostentatiously be paid in any currency in the world, even in gold bars.

Though the Intelligence Services of the great powers are backed by huge amounts of secret Government funds, they quite often face the problem of a shortage of certain currencies. This often happens when an Intelligence Service has overspent its budget and has to improvise until more funds are made available through the slow processes of bureaucracy. The paymaster-spy may then have to arrange ways and means of obtaining a certain currency very quickly, or on the other hand may be instructed to build up a reserve of some such currency in a foreign country.

Several years ago the British needed roubles to operate espionage behind the Iron Curtain. This was ingeniously achieved by smuggling Swiss watches into Russia and thus exchanging them for roubles at a rate very much better than the official rate of exchange.

In the early days of the Soviet Russian regime funds for espionage were scarce and the methods of raising them were often desperate. Sometimes art treasures were looted and sold to raise the currency to send spies abroad. Yagoda, when he was head of the NKVD (Soviet Secret Service) in the early 'thirties used his eventual successor, Lavrentia Beria, to organise the distribution of forged dollar bills through small banks in Germany run by crypto-Communists. This distribution of forged dollar bills was carried out at an ideal time, the era of the bankers' slump and the depression.

Walter Krivitsky, who later escaped to America, was Director of Soviet Espionage in Vienna at the time and he later admitted to the Americans that more than nine million forged dollar bills had been used to finance spying.

When countries are at war the Intelligence Services are sometimes compelled to pick their spies from among people who would normally be ruled out of consideration – even from among the criminal classes. Such a type of spy is the safe-blower and professional burglar.

Not many spies can pick locks and blow safes and when they do almost the only person they can turn to for instruction is the experienced crook. One of the most remarkable crooks to be recruited was Johnny Ramensky, the son of Lithuanian parents born in a Glasgow slum. Prison life began for Johnny when he was sent to Borstal at the age of sixteen. He lived for sixty-seven years and spent more than forty of them in jail.

His speciality in the world of crime was safe-blowing. He was somewhat of a legend in the underworld, not least for his talent for escaping from prison which he did on numerous occasions. Despite his criminal record he was even genuinely liked by the police who called him 'Gentle John'. He never used violence.

In October, 1942, Johnny Ramensky was just finishing one of his spells of imprisonment in Scotland. He was released, taken to London and brought before Brigadier Laycock, then Chief of the Commandos. Soon he was enlisted in that crack detachment of assault troops and asked to make a series of reports on the techniques of safe-blowing.

Johnny was sent to Italy and assigned to a series of missions behind the enemy lines and acting with the Italian Partisans. When the Allies advanced on Rome he accompanied a raiding party whose orders were to secure the German plans for withdrawal. Johnny got the plans after breaking open a safe in the German Embassy. In fact he opened four strong-rooms and ten safes within a few hours.

Usually when spies of this type are recruited – though this is not always the case – they are assigned to a military unit, the idea being that they work best when under Service discipline. This, alas, was only too true of Johnny. When he was demobilised from the Commandos he was given a signed letter by Brigadier Laycock stating 'May your gallant service to King and Country be rewarded in the future by peace, prosperity and happiness'. But shortly after the end of the war Johnny was back in prison again.

'Toni' had a two months' crash course in the espionage game before he was sent into the field. Such training is not given to all agents at an early stage. The usual method is to keep them away from other Secret Service personnel until they have fully proved themselves as being discreet and reliable. In the case of 'Toni' he was being recruited as a specialist agent and therefore needed technical training.

He was, of course, introduced to radio transmitter and receiver sets much more sophisticated than anything he had built himself. 'I was impressed by the efficiency of these sets, but I could not help telling the authorities that my own home-made effort was probably much easier and safer to maintain. After all, if you are in enemy territory, it isn't easy to get spare parts for anything highly technical and probably still on the secret list. This I proved to my own satisfaction in due course'.

During the course he received instruction into a whole series of spy aids and electronic equipment used in espionage. One of the most common of these, which he later had to use on many occasions, was the 'harmonica bug', a tiny, transistorised eavesdropper which can be placed inside an ordinary telephone.

This gadget is easy to carry around and it is activated by a high-pitched note like that of the harmonica after which it is named. 'Toni' was given one of these 'bugs' to test out.

'I was very nervous the first time I tried it', he said, 'and I had some difficulty in fitting it into position on the telephone as my hands were shaking. Once it is fitted, however, all is simple. I dialled the number of the person I was snooping on. The "bug" caused his telephone bell to stop ringing after a couple or so peals and this made him think someone else had dialled a wrong number, discovered the fact and put the phone down.

'Then the "bug" activated a transmitter-receiver mechanism that enabled me not only to listen in to any of the other man's calls, but actually to hear any conversations he might have with other persons within close range of his phone. A frightening development really and only morally justified if used in such a cause as espionage'.

'Toni' was also introduced to the 'radar button' and the 'thermal detector'. The former can pin-point its carrier's position back to base at any given time which means that an agent can be shadowed by his controller and aid sent to him if he is in trouble. The latter makes it possible to discover where people have been sitting or lying and even how many clothes they are wearing.

'They say that this gadget can even distinguish men from women by the swing of their buttocks', 'Toni' told me, 'but I am somewhat doubtful about the accuracy of that claim'.

Bugging devices are nearly all so tiny that they can be hidden in carpet tacks, wall lamps, cigarette packets and inside a bra. The Russians have used them so extensively that periodically all embassies in the Soviet capital have been de-bugged by the security staff, or 'fumigating' as it is sometimes called in the slang of the Intelligence Services.

The gear for de-bugging is rather more formidable than that of bugging and costs far more. It can locate radio microphones and other bugging devices which may be hidden in walls, under desks or conference tables, under floor-boards and on ceilings.

'I must say', said 'Toni', 'that all this instruction was very worthwhile and without it I should never have survived for as long as I have. It also taught me to be alert to the first signs that my own phone might be tapped. The quick two-peal ring, then silence: that is a hint of possible trouble, though it could be just a telephonic fault. Clicking sounds during a telephone conversation can suggest clumsy eavesdropping.

'Later on in the Far East, when I was operating in hostile territory on the borders of Vietnam, I had to experiment with one of the more revolutionary developments of electronic eavesdropping. This is a device known as the CASM, or Computer-controlled Area Sterilisation Multi-Sensor System. This is something which might come right out of the pages of science fiction.

'What happens is that hundreds of small self-contained bugging devices are dropped by aircraft in a certain area. They are of varying sizes, but some are no larger than a full-sized bean. Sensitive to vibration to an uncanny degree, they can pick up the movements of troops or individuals hidden in a jungle, or of tanks and armoured cars.

'My job was to test out this new spy aid and make assessments of its value. In the early stages it was used to investigate movements of enemy scouts between Laos and Vietnam. The jungles in this territory were an ideal testing place'.

CASM has since been developed for strictly military use, though it is still an invaluable aid in spying in certain circumstances. When the 'bugs' are dropped they automatically signal their information to a mobile computer stationed miles away. This provides the military Intelligence with an estimate of the extent of enemy activity under cover of the jungle, whether there are just a few individuals engaged in scouting operations, or if a full-scale assault is being planned. The data enables the robot guns, controlled by radio and computer, to direct fire on to a given area.

Much of today's espionage is directed towards technological improvements and new gadgets produced by commercial firms. It has been through private enterprise and industry that 'bugging' has been developed in recent times rather than by the Secret Services themselves. In fact the latter have had to take steps to keep up with the commercial firms and this has entailed a high degree of commercial espionage carried out by the Intelligence Services.

'Toni' had training not only in all types of bugging, but in the art of de-bugging as well. He was warned that the mere examination of the clothing of a spy does not ensure that he does not possess a mini-bug. These can now be neatly fitted into a filling in a tooth. But the process of de-bugging has been greatly speeded up in recent times : it is now possible to de-bug a room in thirty seconds.

So 'Toni' was shown a whole range of bugging devices so that he should know what to look for and how they could be counteracted. He had to learn about the detector which automatically sweeps through specified radio frequencies to find hidden transmitters, the unit that filters out unwanted background noises, leaving just voices to be bugged, and how to operate a hand-held detector for locating hidden radio transmitters.

A portable, battery-operated
radio transmission detector.
It can detect any radio
transmission between 10
and 250 MHz

A highly sophisticated
American-made telephone
line tapping connection box.
It switches on a tape, only
when the phone is in use

This substitute insert fits into the mouthpiece of a telephone. It is very difficult to detect, it needs no battery and transmits whenever the phone is being used

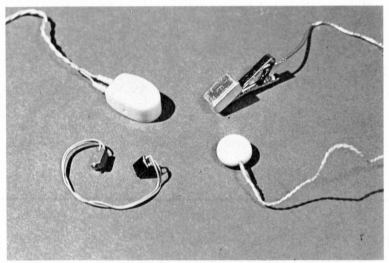

A miniature radio microphone can be fitted into almost anything

A microphone that can actually be fitted into the brickwork of a building

Any spy who fears he may be shadowed or bugged requires a portable detecting kit which will trace hidden wires and metals in a wall, or check strange pulses on electrical circuits. 'The longer you continue safely in this game the greater the odds that somebody has rumbled you and you are being watched', said 'Toni'. 'It is relatively easy in the early stages, because nobody knows or suspects you. But if you remain an agent long enough you must expect somebody will rumble you sooner or later'.

'Toni's' first assignment was in Switzerland. Nothing very exciting happened as this was primarily a test as to how he would react once he was 'in the field'. For two months he posed as a tourist, living in Montreux and paying occasional visits to Geneva and Berne.

'My job then was little more than making discreet contacts with other agents and picking up any worthwhile gossip. I was also asked to assemble a new transmitter-receiver set and, as a test as to my resourcefulness, this had to be done by adaptation and buying spare parts from different shops to avoid suspicion.

'I kept the circuit of the transmitter as simple as possible so that to build it I only required such instruments as a soldering iron, screw driver, pliers and wire strippers. This meant that no sophisticated test equipment was required for adjusting and tuning the transmitter when it was built. All that was needed was a simple multi-meter and a 25-40 watt mains electric light bulb.

'Even so I was at first petrified when I entered a shop to buy even the most unsuspicious equipment. But the transistor radio required little or no modification. I removed the chassis of the mains valve receiver that was to be rebuilt as a transmitter and all the components with the exception of the power supply circuits. The additional components required were the crystal, a tuning condenser (salvaged from another radio receiver) and some copper wire.

'One of the important points I had to remember was the necessity of screening in order to reduce spurious emissions which might interfere with domestic broadcast reception and other radio services. Since most domestic radio receivers are housed in either wooden or plastic cabinets, I had to metalise the case. This I achieved by glueing tinfoil all round the interior of the case, taking care that air vents in the bottom of the case were not covered over'.

'Toni' established contact with other agents purely for test purposes and only on two occasions had to use his set to pass on messages. But, being cautious, and not wishing to be detected in the early stages of his career as a spy, he made it a rule never to transmit for more than six minutes at a time, and never to use it in the same place for more than twice in succession.

After this 'Toni' was moved on to Hong Kong where he was put in charge of a second-hand bookshop as a cover. The premises were de-bugged once a week and he kept a radio transmitter-receiver outfit in the cellar, using this mainly to try to pick up broadcasts from Hanoi and to keep an ear open for any messages that might be passed by foreign agents.

'You can be living in the heart of a huge city, constantly seeing other people and living a gregarious life, but the very fact that you are a spy makes you feel intensely lonely,' was 'Toni's' comment. 'One is constantly on one's guard, never relaxing for long at a time and knowing that if one makes a mistake and gets caught, your own people will disown you.

'In the early days when there was not much happening and I was really employed as a waiting agent, one also had a feeling of guilt that one wasn't really justifying one's existence. This again is somewhat demoralising, yet a good deal of a spy's time is simply waiting and watching'.

Patience, self-sufficiency and self-discipline are the essential attributes of the successful spy. He may appear to live a normal life, but he has to choose his friends carefully and can never ever confide in them. Indeed, sometimes he cannot feel really sure if his employers are to be trusted. This is particularly the case when the spy-masters, as sometimes they do for tactical reasons, give the impression of being suspicious of their own agents. Often these tactics are deliberately adopted to put a spy on his guard.

This is particularly the case with the double-agent whether, like the American we have mentioned previously in this chapter, he infiltrates the enemy with a view to offering his services to his own country, or if he has been captured by the enemy, forced to work for them and then tries to escape to help his own people. I am omitting the case of the double-agent who will serve any power according to the money they give him: he can well take care of himself and has only himself to blame if he comes to grief.

The case of 'Zig-Zag' will illustrate the other type of spy who walks singularly alone and must inevitably feel he is not trusted by either side. His real name was Eddie Chapman, a Briton who had been imprisoned in Jersey in the Channel Islands for safe-blowing and had been taken over by the Germans when they occupied the islands in World War II.

'Zig-Zag' offered his services to the Germans in the hope that they would give him sufficient freedom for him to escape and make his way back to Britain. They accepted his offer, believing that he would have no desire to return to a country where he was regarded as a criminal and listed as such by the police.

Sent to Nantes in France for training in sabotage and radio transmission, he acquired a lot of detailed information about German radio transmissions. In December, 1942, 'Zig-Zag' was dropped by parachute near Ely in England, bringing with him an intelligence questionnaire and a radio set. He immediately gave himself up to the police.

Now it so happened that British Intelligence had a dossier on 'Zig-Zag', even knowing that he could be identified by certain false teeth: a dentist's records gave them all the evidence required to establish his identity. What the British authorities were not sure about was whether he was genuinely on their side or on that of the Germans.

He was frank with the British. He said that the tasks the Germans had set him were to sabotage the de Havilland bomber factory at Hatfield and to send daily weather reports and details about the movement of American troops. The Germans had given him a large amount of money to finance his activities, with the promise of more if he sabotaged the de Havilland works.

'Zig-Zag's' arrival from enemy-occupied territory presented, quite a poser for the British. This brought him into touch with the counter-espionage service known as MI5, the British internal security service which is roughly equivalent to the American FBI (Federal Bureau of Investigation).

One of the aims of a section of MI5 was to persuade enemy agents who were caught in Britain to turn over and work for the Allies. The idea was that while they did this they should still pretend to be working for the enemy and send back bogus reports to them. Naturally this branch of Intelligence kept in close touch with the Secret Service proper and depended on them for reports on enemy agents who might be deflected to the other side.

'Zig-Zag' had both courage and self-sufficiency. He knew how to go it alone and to accept being mistrusted by both sides, with the certain knowledge that if he double-crossed either and was found out he faced death or imprisonment.

The British learned from him that his instructions were to return to Occupied France after he had completed his sabotage. He was to do this either by travelling to Ireland, or by signing up as a seaman and going to Portugal, or by making rendezvous with a German submarine which would be sent to fetch him. The fee he had been promised for the sabotage of the bomber factory was £15,000.

The British sent in camouflage experts to make it appear from the air that there had been a devastating explosion at the de Havilland factory. They knew that if 'Zig-Zag' sent a radio report back to the Germans the latter would probably send reconnaissance planes to obtain aerial photographs to confirm that there had been an explosion. The camouflage was intended to provide confirmation to the aerial photographers.

An agent transmitting at dead of night. 'Toni's' cover here is the second-hand bookshop in Hong Kong

Eddie Chapman, alias 'Zig-Zag'

When 'Zig-Zag' had sent in his false report by radio the British arranged for him to travel as a steward aboard ship to Lisbon where he was to desert and report back to the Germans. He was told exactly what story to tell them by the British Intelligence.

Duly rewarded by the Germans, the double-agent then suggested he should be sent on a sabotage operation to the USA. At the same time he had told the British that he believed he could help organise an underground organisation in France and that, if they agreed, he would be prepared to undertake the assassination of Hitler entirely on his own! The latter offer was declined by the British as being too dangerous and ambitious.

Then in 1944 'Zig-Zag' was again parachuted into England, this time with two radio sets, cameras and a sum of £6,000. The Germans appear to have treated him with less suspicion than the British and to have used him as a consultant in sabotage methods. They had even made him a member of the officers' mess at their headquarters in Nantes.

This time his instructions were to obtain photographs and plans of Britain's Asdic gear for detecting submarines and the radio location system attached to night fighter planes. In addition he was to report on damage caused by flying bombs, the siting of American air force bases and to seek information on a new wireless frequency which the Germans believed was being used against their V-2 weapons.

He was able to give the British a great deal of news of German plans, especially on flying bombs. Once again he was allowed to radio back news to the Germans, this being fed to him by the British who allowed a certain amount of unimportant true information to be sent through as well as many falsehoods.

'Zig-Zag' survived the war successfully, but his daring exploits seem to have gone to his head and he began to show a tendency to boast about them. For this reason he was finally discharged on the grounds of 'lack of security on the part of the agent'.

A German V-2 Rocket

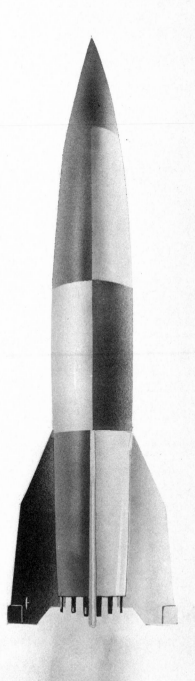

**Samson betrayed by Delilah,
one of the first woman spies**

Chapter 3

How it all started

The spy game is almost as old as man himself. Not that we have much evidence of what the cave men did, but one can make a fair guess that they spied on one another. Probably the oldest hands in espionage are the Chinese who were practising it in a systematic way as early as the fourth century BC.

In the following century the Chinese produced what was the first known text-book on spying, *The Book of War*, by the philosopher Mo Tzu, who advocated a system of 'reporting good and evil to superiors' under which groups of families would be mutually responsible for each other and obliged under penalty of dire punishment to denounce each other's crimes and weaknesses.

Delilah, who clipped Samson's locks, was the forerunner of Mata Hari, one of the earliest of female spies who became an agent of the Philistines. She made her home a hiding place for other Philistine agents and was paid 1,100 pieces of silver for finding out where their enemies were and plotting their destruction.

The Bible is full of spy stories from the time when Moses sent twelve spies into Canaan to the scheming of Rahab the harlot of Jericho who hid the spies of Israel. Indeed, careful students of *The Bible* have learned that it provides quite a few useful lessons in espionage, some of which have been put into practice.

When, in February, 1918, the British Sixtieth Division was ordered by General Allenby to attack Jericho, a brigade major was told to take a detachment to storm a steep hill and capture the village of Michmash. He recalled that Michmash was mentioned in *The Bible* and, looking up Samuel, Book I, chapters 13 and 14, read:

**Margaret Gertrude Zelle,
alias Mata Hari**

. . . the Philistines encamped in Michmash . . . and between the passages, by which Jonathan sought to go over unto the Philistines' garrison, there was a sharp rock on one side, and a sharp rock on the other side: and the name of the one was Bozez and the name of the other Seneh.

The forefront of the one was situate northward over against Michmash, and the other southward over against Gibeah. And Jonathan said to the young man that bare his armour, Come and let us go over unto the garrison . . . it may be that the Lord will work for us: for there is no restraint to the Lord to save by many of by few.

And that first slaughter, which Jonathan and his armour bearer made, was about twenty men, within as it were an half acre of land, which a yoke of oxen might plow.

The young major decided to follow Jonathan's example. He soon discovered that the pass was still exactly as it had been described in the Book of Samuel. Later the major, Vivian Gilbert, was able to report that 'we killed or captured every Turk that night in Michmash, so that after thousands of years the tactics of Saul and Jonathan were repeated with success by a British force'.

While the Chinese were certainly the first people to systematise espionage and extend it to cover the whole community, most of the early spies of history were individualists who ran their own spy services. Alfred the Great may have been absent-minded enough to let the cakes burn, but when it came to spying he was as shrewd and quick-witted as any. Disguising himself as a bard, he stole into the Danes' camp and found out all he needed to know about their strength and dispositions. Alexander the Great heard whispers that his soldiers were discontented with their lot. He thereupon decided to put these rumours to the test. He told his officers that he always kept in touch with his loved ones back at home and urged them to follow his example by writing letters.

Any soldier today hearing such a command from his Commander-in-Chief would immediately be suspicious. But in Alexander's time nobody had ever heard of military censorship so they all wrote home quite freely and those who had moans about the campaign they were fighting and complaints against the Greek Army and Alexander himself set them down quite clearly.

As soon as all the letters had been collected for despatch, Alexander ordered them to be opened and examined. Some soldiers and officers were punished, but, being a general of genius, Alexander was wise enough to note any legitimate complaints and to see things were put right. Censorship can work both ways.

**Alexander the Great. The
inventor of postal
censorship. 334 BC**

The Romans, as one would expect for such an authoritarian nation devoted to law and order, adopted somewhat more sophisticated methods of espionage. They often played on the superstitions of the people they were dealing with. Sertorius, who was the Roman commander in Spain, sent out his spies days before he made an advance against the Iberian tribes. He would not move until he had obtained a mass of intelligence reports. However, wishing to detract attention from his spies and anxious that the enemy should believe he had a supernatural means of acquiring information, he created a legend around the white fawn which was his pet.

Sertorius trained this fawn to follow him wherever he went, giving it signals when to stop and when to come forward. Whenever there was a trial and a verdict was required, Sertorius would signal his fawn to come up to the tribunal and stand close to him. Then he would bend down towards the fawn as though listening to it, after which he would deliver his verdict.

The Iberian tribesmen were convinced that Sertorius consulted his pet fawn and was in some way given supernatural advice by this means.

Omar Sharif, as Genghis Khan surrounded by his warriors

The pigeon and even the swallow were used as couriers in the early stages of espionage and herein probably lies the secret of the speed of communications which the Roman armies possessed. But Genghis Khan, when he began his victorious campaign across Asia, relied on horses for obtaining his information quickly. He was the first general in history to develop espionage on something approaching modern lines.

Genghis never made an attack without first of all getting detailed information about the town, community or territory which he proposed to conquer. He sent out his spies on horseback and ordered them to make friends with the people he was about to attack, to win their confidence and glean intelligence of their strength. Marco Polo reported that these spies travelled as much as 250 miles in a day and that they were 'highly prized and could never do it did they not bind hard the stomach, head and chest with string bands'.

Sometimes Genghis Khan sent merchant-spies with his couriers, using them to barter goods for information. Often these spies kidnapped informers and brought them back to Genghis's camp. When they occupied a new territory in their drive across Asia into Europe the followers of Genghis Khan taught the natives how to spy. Some historians take the view that it was due to the teaching of the Mongol invaders that Russia became such a spy-conscious nation, a trait that has lasted throughout the centuries.

The French were one of the first European countries to introduce a secret police system. This was established by King Charles in the fourteenth century. Intended to defend

**Cardinal Wolsey. One of
Henry VIII's statesmen and
an early spy master**

the realm, it swiftly degenerated into a system of oppression, robbing citizens of their liberties.

In Britain King Edward I created something even more odious when in a Statute of 1285 he introduced the profession of 'State Informer'. This again was intended to keep a watch on suspicious foreigners and to smell out sedition, but by the very nature of the appointment it was open to abuse. The 'State Informer' was paid twenty pounds plus one-half of the belongings of any person convicted on his testimony.

The medieval Church had by far the most widespread and efficient espionage service of its day. No single nation could compete with it in this respect. Indeed, at a later stage of history individual nations very often chose princes of the Church as their own organisers in the spy game, Cardinal Wolsey in England and Cardinal Richelieu in France being notable examples.

The Church's great weapon in breaking down its victims was the Inquisition, which achieved its greatest notoriety in Spain where the Grand Inquisitor, Frey Tomas de Torquemada, brought in the torture chamber for 'examining' suspected heretics.

It was, of course, a brutal, savage age, but terrible as were the deeds wrought by the Inquisition, the paradox is that the Inquisitors themselves were devout, incorruptible men who never sought to profit personally from their persecutions. Torquemada, for example, imposed on himself a life of poverty and austerity, never eating meat and never even having linen on his bed.

Yet it was a heresy in those days to suggest that the earth went round the sun. And it was to root out people who had such beliefs, or worse, who might argue that the earth was not flat, that spies were trained by the Church.

One of the rules laid down by the Church for its spies, published in Rome in 1585, was as follows:

Be it noted that the spy, simulating friendship and seeking to draw from the accused a confession of his crime, may very well pretend to be of the sect of the accused, but he must not say so, because in saying so he would at least commit a venial sin, and we know that much must not be committed upon any grounds whatever.

**One method of torturing a
spy into telling secrets**

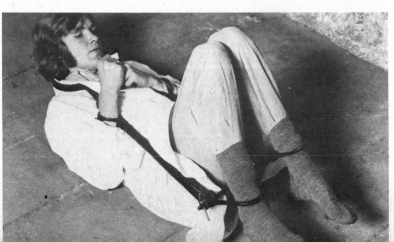

In civil courts, even in those days, confession of a crime alone was not sufficient to obtain a conviction: there had to be independent proof. In the Church courts a confession alone was sufficient which, unhappily, explained many of the 'confessions' obtained under torture.

The sixteenth century saw the development of espionage in Europe into national Secret Services. In England the man who became the father of the Secret Service was Sir Francis Walsingham, a man so dedicated to the cause of his country that he frequently spent his own personal money on building up a spy network when his sovereign, Queen Elizabeth, would not grant him the funds.

Spain represented the greatest threat to England in that period and Walsingham concentrated all his efforts to obtaining information on Spain's plans. Almost any eager, adventurous, well educated young man, prepared to travel

Sir Francis Walsingham. Director of Intelligence for Elizabeth I

abroad, could get a job as a spy for Walsingham. He encouraged students to go abroad and report back to him.

Walsingham gave them grants of a hundred pounds a year, sending them mainly to Italy where at Venice and other ports they were able to pick up details of Spanish plots, troop and ship movements.

It was these brilliant young men who enabled Walsingham to build up a detailed picture of the organisation of the Spanish Armada and the Spanish King's plans to invade England. Much of the money for financing the Armada came from bankers in Genoa. Walsingham discovered who they were and bribed them to delay sending money to Spain. All this gave England more time to prepare against the Armada.

Sir Francis was the first man in England to establish a code-breaking team. He picked his men from among mathematicians and the Universities and guided them

Elizabeth I

personally. As a young man he had studied cryptography and on a visit to the continent had brought back a book on the subject by one Alberti.

His London home became the centre for the code and cipher readers and it was also the place in which he trained his spies. At one time he had as many as fifty-three spies on the continent, a remarkably large number for this era.

Through the interception of coded messages smuggled to Mary Queen of Scots in her captivity, Walsingham was able to break a plot by her supporters to assassinate Queen Elizabeth. But Mary's followers always claimed that the coded messages were forgeries done by Walsingham himself in order to get rid of her.

History shows that the Phoenicians were the first race to practise commercial espionage, but this art seems to have been neglected by the European powers when they began to

Mary Queen of Scots. Her letters were intercepted by Walsingham

Oliver Cromwell. His spy network was the best in the world

Samuel Pepys. Secretary to the Admiralty as well as being a writer

Daniel Defoe, alias Alexander Goldsmith, Claude Guilot. 'Father of the British Secret Service'

Robert Harley, Earl of Oxford

Lord Godolphin

organise their Secret Services. By the early sixteenth century France was easily in the lead with the most efficient Intelligence service in Europe, with Holland second and England trailing a rather poor third.

After Walsingham's death there was no one of his calibre to replace him. In Venice, which then had its own government, laws were passed to make spying not merely difficult, but dangerous. Death or lifelong imprisonment was the penalty for any of its officials seen speaking to a Foreign Minister or Ambassador.

Bribery was the chief weapon of the rival Secret Services. It is recorded that the Spanish viceroy of Naples spent 50,000 ducats on 'secret expenses' in 1612. Louis XIV spent more than seven times that figure in bribing the Germanic princes in preparing for war against Austria and Holland.

'Well chosen spies contribute more than any other agency to the success of great plans', wrote Francois de Callières, a seventeenth century French diplomat. 'There is no expense better designed than that which is laid out upon a secret service. It would be inexcusable for a Minister of State to neglect it'.

Richelieu and Mazarin, two Cardinals, were largely responsible for putting France in the forefront in espionage in the early seventeenth century. But when Cromwell came to power in England he set about re-organising the Secret Service by putting John Thurloe in charge of it.

Samuel Pepys wrote in his famous Diary that Cromwell spent '£70,000 annually for intelligence ... thereby Cromwell carried the secrets of all the princes of Europe at his girdle'.

Certainly England had one of the finest Intelligence Services in Europe in this period. Thurloe had agents at every court and as Postmaster-General he intercepted correspondence from abroad.

Perhaps the greatest tribute to Cromwell's spy network was that paid by the Venetian Ambassador to England, one Sagredo.

Certainly no Government on earth discloses its own acts less and knows those of others more precisely than that of England. They meet in a room approached through others, without number, and countless doors are shut . . . To discover the affairs of others they do not employ ambassadors, but use spies, as less conspicuous, making use of men of spirit, but without rank, unlikely to be noticed.

It was a message from an agent as far afield as Jamaica which enabled Cromwell to know exactly the disposition and movements of the Spanish plate-fleet and so resulted in Admiral Blake capturing it at Tenerife.

One of the most extensive spying missions attempted was that ordered by Louis XIV in 1685 when he sent Captain Gravier d'Ortières to Constantinople. The instructions given to d'Ortières were that he was to assemble a team of skilled officers, including engineers, to make a secret and detailed survey of the Dardanelles, the coasts of Asia Minor, Syria and Egypt.

This mission did not end until 1687 and the findings of the spies, including maps, filled three volumes and was entitled 'The State of the Places which the Mohammedan princes possess on the coasts of the Mediterranean Sea and which Plans have been made by the Order of the King under Cover of the Visit to the Levantine Seaports, 1686 and 1687, with the Project of making a Descent and becoming Masters of them'.

Unfortunately for d'Ortières he had taken the trouble to work out in detail the cost of an expedition to bring this project to a successful conclusion. The total sum was 31,787, 940 livres. The King considered it was too great an expense to win new territory.

History books do not give him the credit for it, but Daniel Defoe, the author of *Robinson Crusoe*, was a key man in the British Secret Service in the early part of the eighteenth century.

He was an unlikely choice for such a role. Rebel, revolutionary pamphleteer, twice imprisoned and put in the pillory, Defoe himself nevertheless admitted that he had been employed by Queen Anne 'in several honourable, though secret services'.

It was not an empty boast. He was highly regarded by Robert Harley, Earl of Oxford, who saw in Defoe a trained and meticulous observer who could put into coherent form and with a wealth of detail all he saw and heard. Harley obtained Defoe's release from prison and the Harley Papers make it abundantly clear that Defoe worked as a secret agent under both Harley and Lord Godolphin.

Even more remarkably Lord Godolphin, when forced out of office by Queen Anne in 1710, recommended Defoe to be his successor. His chief talent as far as espionage was concerned seems to have been an ability for discovering the hiding-places of Jacobites.

Defoe, emboldened by his success, wrote to Harley, urging the creation of a new secret service for England, by which the Queen's Ministers could be provided with intelligence from all parts of the kingdom.

As a result he was sent on a tour of the country as the principal secret agent, organising other spies as he went along, travelling incognito, sometimes as 'Alexander Goldsmith' and at others as 'Claude Guilot'. He posed as a writer during his travels and his book, *Tour Through England*

and Wales, was a lucrative sideline to his espionage. He seems to have revelled in intrigue for its own sake.

In the eighteenth century spying gradually developed on rather more original lines and less reliance was put on bribery and mere powers of observation. Women began to play a role in the spy game which they had not enjoyed since the time of Delilah. There was the Marquise de Pompadour, mistress of Louis XV, who made one of her favourites chief of the secret police on the understanding that he discovered all the gossip about her that was going the rounds.

Probably more time was wasted on finding out this kind of tittle-tattle than in obtaining worthwhile information, but the Marquise was a power in the land and she largely decided who were sent as spies to foreign courts.

Perhaps the significance which was attached to women being able to worm out secrets may be gleaned in an unorthodox way by the use made of one of the most bizarre spies of his age, the Chevalier Charles Geneviève Louis Auguste André Timothée d'Eon de Beaumont.

This slim, elegant young man had been dressed by his mother as a girl up to the age of seven. He was said to have pretty, girlish looks, but he was a courageous, clever youth whose ability as a fencer brought him fame early on. Then Louis XV hit on the idea of getting the Chevalier to dress up as a girl and to go to the Russian court as 'Mlle. Lia de Beaumont'.

He took with him a book inside which was cunningly concealed a letter from Louis XV to the Czarina Elizabeth. In the letter was a secret cipher which the Czarina was to use to correspond with the French court. It was a tricky assignment for any novice spy, for the Russian court was a hive of intrigue, with the Czarina alleged to be pro-French and anti-British and the Chancellor, Bestuchev, pro-British and anti-French.

D'Eon de Beaumont played his part admirably. His disguise deceived everyone, including the court painters who clamoured to do his portrait, and once or twice he had to ward off some impetuous suitors. Finding an ally in the Vice-Chancellor, Vonontzov, the young Chevalier was through him presented to the Czarina.

Soon he was appointed maid of honour to the aged Czarina and it is a tribute to his influence that shortly after the appointment a disconsolate British Ambassador was writing home to say that the Chancellor could not persuade the Czarina to sign a treaty with Britain.

Whether d'Eon de Beaumont eventually revealed his true identity to the Czarina is not known for certain, but he probably did. It is said that the Czarina offered him an important post at her court, but that he declined and returned to France.

The Chevalier had a long and exciting career as a spy and was for some years well rewarded for his work. Yet, while he was away in London, again working for his French masters, intrigues against him seem to have been launched in Paris. Ultimately d'Eon refused to return to France when ordered to do so and spent his remaining years living in exile in England.

Curiously d'Eon unwittingly played a part in America's fight for independence. Through his friend, John Wilkes, the rakish Radical Member of Parliament, the Chevalier was introduced to Arthur Lee, who then represented the American colonies in London. He in turn brought together Lee and Caron de Beaumarchais, another secret agent named as an envoy to London by Louis XVI.

Lee and de Beaumarchais soon established a close working relationship which led to the supply of arms and other goods to the American insurgents against the English Crown. One can say that the first experience of espionage gained by America was in the days of the prolonged war against England during which it became essential to have secret agents in both Britain and France and, to a lesser extent, in Germany.

There is perhaps no war which creates so much bitterness and suspicion as a civil war and the War of Independence was no exception. Spy mania developed in both camps with British and Americans each professing to find traitors in their own ranks. Even the great Benjamin Franklin, one of the father-founders of American independence, was suspected of passing information to the English.

George Washington developed his own intelligence service during the war and, though numerically his spies were fewer than on the English side, he was greatly aided by the fanaticism and enthusiasm of his agents. He deputed Major Benjamin Tallmadge to organise his Secret Service and, to

Benjamin Franklin. One of the father-founders of American Independence

George Washington. 1st President of the United States of America

guard against accidents, he named Robert Townsend as his number two.

The task of these two men was doubly dangerous because, unlike most spy-masters, they posted themselves right in the front line – in the port of New York, which was the English military base and supply point. Townsend used as his 'cover' a general stores where he managed to elicit information from English customers in a most ingenuous manner.

In those early days of American secret service a very primitive code of signals was devised, comprising such simple materials as a black petticoat and handkerchiefs. The former was hoisted on a clothes line to signal the arrival of the courier at Long Island Sound.

But subtler methods were used by other supporters of the American revolution. James Madison, writing to Edmund Randolph, with whom he was conducting secret correspondence, stated that the key to a new cipher would be 'the name of a certain black servant boy who used to wait on Mr James Madison'. The name was Cupid and it was written at the head of five columns of letters with an alphabet in succession beneath each letter and set of numbers paralleling the lines.

No doubt it sounds a complicated cipher. So it proved to be. Madison made so many errors in writing messages with it that Randolph was unable to decipher them. He had to beg Madison to repeat the messages in plain English. Madison's original messages in cipher have since been examined by modern code and cipher breakers, but they have all failed to translate them. Yet, basically, Madison's system was sound and simple once the principles were grasped.

Townsend remained until the end the key man in the Intelligence service of the revolutionaries. When George Washington became President of the United States he remembered his Secret Service agents and he gave orders that they were to be looked after and that no harm should ever come to them. He also gave orders that all documents relating to their work were to remain secret for an indefinite period.

Chapter 4

The multi-million dollar American espionage industry

No espionage service in the whole of history has cost so much as that of the Central Intelligence Agency of the United States. It is more than just a mere intelligence-collecting service: in effect it is a vast multi-million dollar industry comparable to General Motors, extending all over the world and employing a large number of personnel.

All told, espionage, if you include the intelligence services of the American armed forces, aerial reconnaissance and the use of satellites in the sky for spying, is now probably costing the United States something like 5,000,000,000 dollars a year. In 1967, when many probing questions were asked by Congress members about this spending, it was officially admitted that CIA costs alone were at the rate of 1,500,000,000 dollars a year.

For many years – certainly from the late nineteenth century until towards the end of World War II Russia led the world in espionage spending. Today it can safely be said that the United States has long since surpassed the Soviet Union in this respect, though without doubt Soviet Russia spends more on its internal intelligence network – i.e. on watching its own citizens.

American intelligence really began in the War of Independence, when, as we have already seen, General Washington not only ordered the organisation of a spy network to operate against the British, but a counter-espionage system as well. This organisation was kept alive in a small way and after the war mainly directed against the British, who were suspected of having designs on Florida with a view to setting up a naval base there.

In these early days the American spy system was often operated by desperadoes and men of doubtful character who mixed their spying with a good deal of villainy and dubious deals for personal gain. There was Jean Lafitte, who spied

**Some comments of the
Press on the CIA**

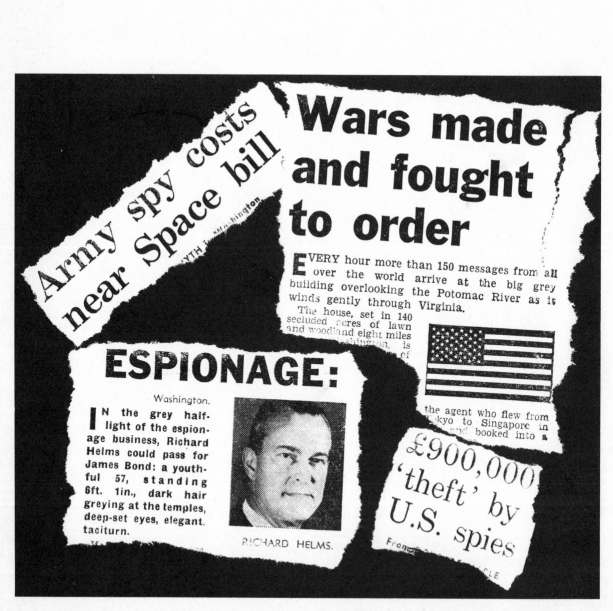

Army spy costs near Space bill
...YTH in Washington

Wars made and fought to order

EVERY hour more than 150 messages from all over the world arrive at the big grey building overlooking the Potomac River as it winds gently through Virginia.

The house, set in 140 secluded acres of lawn and woodland eight miles ...shington. is ...of

ESPIONAGE:

Washington.

IN the grey half-light of the espionage business, Richard Helms could pass for James Bond: a youthful 57, standing 6ft. 1in., dark hair greying at the temples, deep-set eyes, elegant. taciturn.

RICHARD HELMS.

the agent who flew from ...kyo to Singapore in ...and booked into a

£900,000 'theft' by U.S. spies

Franc...

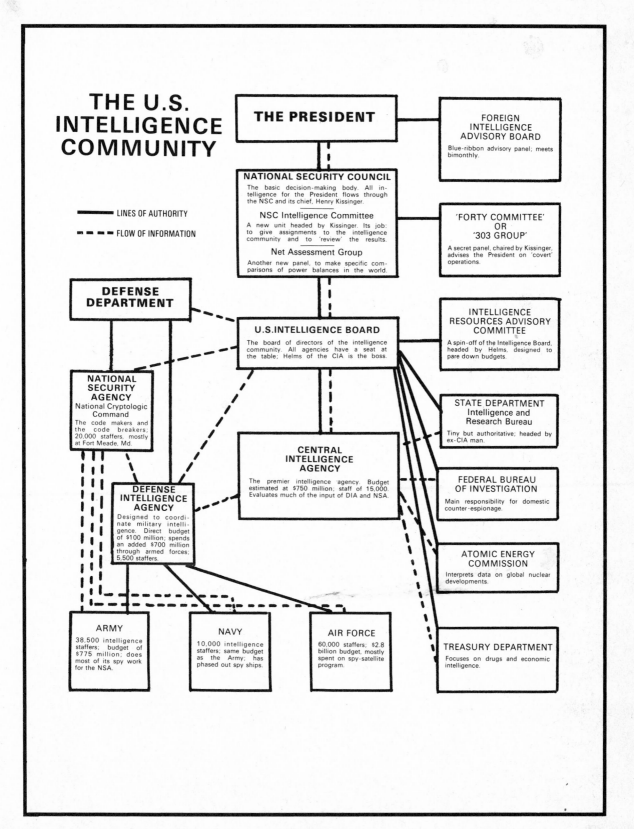

THE U.S. INTELLIGENCE COMMUNITY

LINES OF AUTHORITY

FLOW OF INFORMATION

THE PRESIDENT

FOREIGN INTELLIGENCE ADVISORY BOARD

Blue-ribbon advisory panel; meets bimonthly.

NATIONAL SECURITY COUNCIL

The basic decision-making body. All intelligence for the President flows through the NSC and its chief, Henry Kissinger.

NSC Intelligence Committee

A new unit headed by Kissinger. Its job: to give assignments to the intelligence community and to 'review' the results.

Net Assessment Group

Another new panel, to make specific comparisons of power balances in the world.

'FORTY COMMITTEE' OR '303 GROUP'

A secret panel, chaired by Kissinger, advises the President on 'covert' operations.

DEFENSE DEPARTMENT

U.S. INTELLIGENCE BOARD

The board of directors of the intelligence community. All agencies have a seat at the table; Helms of the CIA is the boss.

INTELLIGENCE RESOURCES ADVISORY COMMITTEE

A spin-off of the Intelligence Board, headed by Helms, designed to pare down budgets.

NATIONAL SECURITY AGENCY

National Cryptologic Command

The code makers and the code breakers; 20,000 staffers, mostly at Fort Meade, Md.

STATE DEPARTMENT Intelligence and Research Bureau

Tiny but authoritative; headed by ex-CIA man.

CENTRAL INTELLIGENCE AGENCY

The premier intelligence agency. Budget estimated at $750 million; staff of 15,000. Evaluates much of the input of DIA and NSA.

FEDERAL BUREAU OF INVESTIGATION

Main responsibility for domestic counter-espionage.

DEFENSE INTELLIGENCE AGENCY

Designed to coordinate military intelligence. Direct budget of $100 million; spends an added $700 million through armed forces; 5,500 staffers.

ATOMIC ENERGY COMMISSION

Interprets data on global nuclear developments.

ARMY

38,500 intelligence staffers; budget of $775 million; does most of its spy work for the NSA.

NAVY

10,000 intelligence staffers; same budget as the Army; has phased out spy ships.

AIR FORCE

60,000 staffers; $2.8 billion budget, mostly spent on spy-satellite program.

TREASURY DEPARTMENT

Focuses on drugs and economic intelligence.

for General Andrew Jackson and won quite a reputation for his reports on British activities in Florida and the Gulf of Mexico.

Lafitte more or less established his personal rule in Galveston and terrorised the neighbourhood. Hearing that the Governor of Louisiana had offered a reward of 5,000 dollars for his capture and execution, he hit back by promising 50,000 dollars for the Governor's head!

Another of his projects was to rescue Napoleon from his exile in St. Helena, but by the time he was ready to attempt this the 'Little Emperor' was already dying.

During the Civil War espionage curiously enough was conducted in a somewhat desultory and amateurish fashion, very different from the professionalism on which General Washington had insisted. It was in this period that the Government called in Allan Pinkerton, founder of the great

Napoleon, Lafitte's 'Little Emperor'

detective agency, to assist them. Later Pinkerton, by going to Baltimore under an assumed name and circulating among notorious Seccessionist plotters, discovered a plot to assassinate Abraham Lincoln. He saved Lincoln's life on that occasion by giving a timely warning, but, despite this, the President remained obstinately opposed to being surrounded by guards, and this was the chief reason why he finally succumbed to an assassin's bullet in 1865.

Eventually Allan Pinkerton became the first chief of the Federal Secret Service and he put espionage on a firm professional basis for the first time. But the service in those days was really quite a small affair and many of the agents were of poor quality. Perhaps the most celebrated and romantic spy of this era was on the side of the Rebels. She was Belle Boyd, the daughter of a Federal official in Virginia.

Abraham Lincoln's assassination in the theatre 1865

This pert, pretty girl in her crinolines and lace was only seventeen when invading Federal forces forced their way into her home and insulted her mother. Belle was so enraged that she took a pistol and shot dead one of the Federal sergeants. On that occasion her youthfulness and the fact that she was a female saved her from punishment.

Belle Boyd

From that day on Belle volunteered as a spy for the Rebels. She collected information, ventured far afield into the enemy lines and beyond, and on several occasions brought back intelligence of great value. She seems to have used her charm and femininity to devastating effect, not only in obtaining information, but in bewitching her enemies. Even when she was captured, Abraham Lincoln himself intervened to prevent her being subjected to the death penalty.

'The most famous woman concerned with official secret activities in the Civil War' is how Belle's biographer, Joseph Hergesheimer, described her. Napoleon, before he made any decision about promoting his senior officers, always asked them: 'But are you lucky?' This question might well be applied to spies. Certainly luck plays a part in their survival and Belle was unquestionably lucky. Making little effort to disguise herself on her forays behind the enemy lines, she often came under fire and seems to have relied solely on her persuasive charms. In captivity she used the same tactics on her warders, though not always quite so successfully. Eventually she was exchanged for another prisoner, travelled the world, married and later gave lectures on her experiences as a spy.

During the American – Spanish War at the end of the last century a young American, who had just graduated from West Point Military Academy, was recruited into the Secret Service by the kind of lucky chance which would have been impossible today. Though he had never been to Cuba, he had written a book about the island which suggested he had a wealth of knowledge about its interior. The American authorities were anxious to have more detailed information on Cuba and, on the strength of his having had this book published, Rowan was commissioned to go there to seek out the insurgent leader, General Garcia, and find out what aid he required.

Not only did Rowan establish contacts with the Cuban insurgents, but obtained details about the strength and dispositions of the Spanish forces and in due course met General Garcia. By travelling mostly by night and hiding from the Spanish forces by day Rowan was able to escape from Cuba and bring back what proved to be vital intelligence. Yet if the Americans had known in the first place that he had never been to Cuba, his eventual promotion to lieutenant-colonel might never have been achieved.

In World War I the American Secret Service was still not comparable in size and scope with that of their other chief allies. Between 1918 and 1939 the most important development in American counter-espionage was the drive against Nazi saboteurs by the Federal Bureau of Investigation. But for the FBI it is possible that Nazi Germany could have wrought great havoc with subversive agents inside the United States. In the 'thirties the Germans poured secret funds into America to support their agents and because of the large number of German-born people in the USA it was not difficult for them to establish a bridgehead.

The FBI made a late start against these operations, but once they were given greater financial backing their professional agents vigorously set about tracking down Nazi spy-nests and undercover organisations.

The key man in all this was J Edgar Hoover, the tough and frighteningly ferocious chief of the FBI. Starting life as a clerk at ten dollars a week, Hoover later took a job as a messenger in the Library of Congress while studying at night for a law degree. After graduating he went to work as an attorney in the Department of Justice and it was through his legal experience that he was eventually chosen at the early age of twenty-nine as chief of the FBI.

Hoover became a legend in his life-time and not only one of the most important and powerful men in the United States, but sometimes a man to whom not even the President dared say no. First of all he directed his attention to fighting the organised gangster, but as war approached he turned his attention increasingly to counter-espionage and began to create the finest and largest spy-hunting army America has ever had. It was under his direction that in World War II 16,000 enemy aliens were rounded up, ten German saboteurs caught and a 33-man spy-ring in New York was broken up by using hidden film cameras and a 'look-through trick mirror'.

It was as well that America possessed so tough and zealous a spy-catcher as Edgar Hoover in those years because it must be admitted that the nation's Secret Service was not only below par in strength, but in personnel, too. The vital department was the Office of Strategic Services (known for short as the OSS), but even this was a small organisation when the disaster of Pearl Harbour occurred and forced the Government to realise the need for an enlarged Secret Service.

Just as the FBI owed almost everything to the drive of one man, Hoover, so the OSS was improved out of all recognition by Major-General William J ('Wild Bill') Donovan. Like Hoover, Donovan had also had legal training as well as being a soldier.

President Roosevelt had personally asked Donovan to take charge of the OSS in the summer of 1941. 'You have a

J Edgar Hoover. Director of the FBI from 1924

gigantic task in front of you,' said the President. 'There is straw, but no bricks to build with, for to all intents and purposes we just don't possess a Secret Service.'

There was some rivalry between the OSS and the FBI and Hoover regarded the whole of America, north, central and south as his own province. As a compromise it was agreed that the FBI would carry out all operations in the Americas, but that Donovan should be assigned the rest of the world.

Recruitment went ahead at great speed and for those who may wonder whether their own particular qualifications fit them for the spy game it is interesting to note the variety of jobs held by newcomers to the OSS. Many were foreign-born and had fluency in languages, some were professors and teachers, others included circus artists, cowboys, acrobatic stunt-men, while there were also bartenders, night-club operators, deep-sea divers, missionaries, forgers, safe-busters, locksmiths and even members of the Mafia.

In fact, especially members of the Mafia. Many people since have criticised Donovan and others for adopting a deliberate policy of recruiting Mafia gangsters for the Secret Service, but it was nevertheless a brilliant ploy on Donovan's part and to a large extent it worked one of the espionage miracles of World War II. In retrospect it can be said that by recruiting the Mafia the Americans ensured the speedy success of the invasion of Sicily and so paved the way for the down-fall of Mussolini, the Italian dictator.

Two simple facts became obvious to Donovan and from them he made all the right deductions. The first was that Mussolini had effectively stamped out the Mafia not only in Italy, but in its chief centre – Sicily. Many key men in the Mafia had gone to the United States to start up operations there; some of them were behind bars.

Charles 'Lucky' Luciano in Naples

Firefighters work on a blazing battleship at Pearl Harbour

'Wild Bill' Donovan in disguise

**Benito Mussolini. 1883-1945.
Giving the Fascist Salute**

Therefore, argued Donovan, Mussolini was not popular
with the Mafia and they felt they had a score to pay off
against him. Now if the United States were to let some of
these key Mafia men out of jail and smuggled them into
Sicily, the OSS could establish a Trojan horse on Italian
territory.

It was a logical plan, it appealed to the military and offered
a real chance of winning a major battle in the Mediterranean
theatre of the war. Of course there were risks, but Donovan
thought they were worth taking.

Mussolini had determined to get rid of the Mafia because
he feared that as an organisation it might pose a threat to his
own Fascist Party. So he had ordered a round-up of thousands
of suspects and had them shipped off to penal islands.

'Lucky' Luciano at his desk in Naples

Troops in Sicily. A column on the road near Catania

The key members of the Mafia were, however, too clever for the Italian dictator. Some joined the Fascist Party, kept the secret of their Mafia membership and laid low. Others fled to the USA.

The head of the Mafia in America was Salvatore Lucania, better known as 'Lucky' Luciano and one of the most dangerous gangsters in the United States. He had been sent to prison to serve a 35-years sentence when in 1943 the Secret Service, aided and abetted by the US Navy, had him released. The Secret Service used him to establish contact with the remnants of the Mafia in Sicily. It was said that he was taken to Sicily by the US Navy and seen in the vicinity of the US Seventh Army shortly after the American troops landed there in the summer of 1943.

What is certain, even though this whole operation is still somewhat shrouded in mystery, is that by using the Mafia the Americans were able not only to speedily occupy the whole of Sicily, but to have a ready-made pro-Allied local administration set up there within a matter of weeks, if not days.

While the British and Canadian troops had a tough task against the strongest German units in fighting up the east coast of Sicily, taking them five weeks to reach the key port of Messina, the Americans, thanks to Mafia secret agents, were able to occupy the western side of the island and the mountainous areas in seven days. Here they were aided by one Don Calo, a Mafia leader. It is said that when Don Calo was appointed Mayor of Villalba by the American Officer of Civilian Affairs, he shouted 'Long live the Allies! Long live the Mafia!'

If you are a keen amateur photographer with a large
collection of films or snapshots of foreign countries, especially
of lonely bays and stretches of the coast, never, ever discard
these. One day they may enable you to play a vital role in the
spy game. The OSS made a great reputation for itself in
World War II by its unequalled collection of large-scale maps
of enemy territories, or territories occupied by the enemy.
These were compiled not simply from adapting existing maps,
but by providing the cartographers with collections of
photographs of the terrain.

Throughout World War II it was an axiom of all military
thinking on the part of the Allies that the enemy could only
be defeated by landing troops along vast stretches of coast-
line. Big, conventional ships could not make such landings;
the task was given to the thousands of flat-bottomed landing-
craft which could easily touch down on gently sloping beaches.

Thus photographs were helpful to reveal the nature of these
beaches at different states of the tide, to show whether they
had gentle slopes, whether the shore was sandy or strewn
with rocks, as the latter could cut a boat to pieces. More
important, too, photographs showing landmarks on the shore –
a church, a tower, or even a farmhouse – enabled landing-
craft to fix their position on good landing points as quite
often only a very short stretch of beach would be suitable
for the landing-craft to negotiate.

The jobs which OSS men had to do inside enemy territory
during the war were varied and surprising. Two men were
smuggled into French West Africa, then held by the Vichy
French, and, on the strength of their knowledge of the
German language made contact with German Intelligence.
They were able to plant faked documents on the Germans,
suggesting that 'Operation Tropical' had been planned with
the aim of landing Allied forces in the Dakar area. As a result

**Troops going ashore in
Sicily**

the Germans took the 'warning' seriously and summoned up
their naval forces to lie off Dakar in wait for the arrival of the
assault force. No such invasion fleet arrived. Instead the
Allied landings along the Moroccan and Algerian coasts
(for long secretly planned as 'Operation Torch'), nearly
2,000 miles distant, took place at that very moment,
unhindered by any serious naval opposition.

Yet the most brilliant success in American espionage in
this period was achieved in Switzerland where Allen Dulles,
later to become chief of the Central Intelligence Agency, was
OSS representative in Berne.

Dulles was a skilled and resourceful spy-master with a
great gift for character-reading. So hard did he work in this
neutral capital that he built up a network of informants not
only in Switzerland itself, but extending to Germany, Spain,
Portugal, Yugoslavia, Bulgaria and North Africa. This
achievement was all the more remarkable in that Dulles
himself was suspected of being the master-mind of American
intelligence in the area and was therefore constantly watched
by German agents and even had one of them infiltrated into
his household as a cook.

Because Dulles was suspected of being an American
Intelligence chief information began to flow into his office
by devious means. Some of it was unimportant and merely
the attempt of amateurs to earn a few extra dollars, a good
deal was false intelligence deliberately planted by the enemy.
Dulles' problems were to assess what was worthwhile and
what was worthless and to decide which would-be agents were
genuine and which were planted by the Germans. This was
no easy task for a newly created Intelligence unit.

Then in August, 1943, a German who claimed to work in
the German Foreign Office, slipped across the border into
Switzerland, and offered a mass of highly confidential
documents, all of them obtained from the Foreign Office.
It all seemed too good to be true and yet there was nothing
in the papers to suggest they were other than authentic.

The unexpected visitor's story was that he was an anti-Nazi
and would like nothing better than to see Hitler's regime
overthrown and peace made with the United States. Dulles
decided to take a risk. He gave his visitor a code name,
'George Wood', which he was to use when he was able to
contact any other American embassies, offices or legations on
his travels around Europe.

'George Wood' turned out to be that rarity in the spy
world, an idealist who was not out for personal gain and who,
at the same time, was in a position to produce valuable
information. Soon from various points in Europe material
began to flow in from this newly recruited agent. There was
information about how tungsten was being smuggled into
Germany from Spain in crates of oranges, of a new secret

German radio station, of troop movements and details of diplomatic cables.

Most important of all was the discovery by 'George Wood' that Elyesa Bazna, the butler to the British Ambassador in Turkey, was a German agent who had obtained the combination to the Ambassador's safe, was photographing documents he found in it and passing them on to the Germans. This spy was the notorious 'Cicero'. It was through 'George Wood' that Dulles was able to warn the British of the spy in their embassy.

The OSS, after a somewhat disappointing start, also scored a number of successes in China in World War II. One of the problems in the early stages was the lack of Chinese specialists and agents who spoke the language; the other was that the Chinese wanted to control American espionage.

There was no area of the world where spying was made so difficult as in China where among the Chinese themselves there were several rival Secret Services, that of the Communists, Chiang-Kai-shek's own organisation, the dreaded secret agency of General Tai Li and various smaller, rival intelligence bodies all spying on each other.

The OSS had to try to work to some extent with all these different agencies in that in varying degrees they were all supposed to be fighting the Japanese. This task was not made any easier by the fact that some of them were rather keener on spying on each other than in tackling the enemy.

The OSS agents had two main roles, apart from gathering intelligence. One was to recruit and train guerrilla groups, the other was to use psychological warfare and where possible to infiltrate the Japanese armies with the aim of spreading demoralisation.

One of the ablest members of the OSS was Oliver J Caldwell, an American born in China, who had studied at Nanking University. He volunteered for service with the OSS after Pearl Harbour and, when he went to China, found himself in a tangled web of espionage through which he had to pick his path with caution.

'All this time,' he wrote afterwards, 'I was, in effect, a triple agent. I was an American army officer assigned to OSS, which had detailed me to Tai Li's Secret Military Police. With the approval of my OSS colonel, I worked through Mr Chen with the secret societies which were now dedicated to overthrowing Chiang Kai-shek and Tai Li.'

There were no spectacular coups for the OSS in China, but it is probably true to say that the experience gained in operating in this vast, diverse and complex country formed the basis for the creation of the Central Intelligence Agency after the war. The OSS agents were brave, endured great hardships, ran many risks and gained a real insight into the problems of China's future.

Alas, their reports were largely ignored. The OSS was a new organisation and therefore suffered from the jealousies and in some cases downright obstructiveness of rival intelligence bodies, particularly in the Services. Had more attention been paid to them back in Washington the triumph of Mao Tse-tung and his Communist followers might never have occurred. The OSS agents warned that the Chinese Communists were ruthless, efficient, disciplined and gaining ground, though still distrusted by the vast majority of Chinese, but that the forces of Chiang Kai-shek were corrupt, inefficient and rapidly alienating themselves from moderate opinion among China's silent and uncommitted millions.

The OSS message was clear: the United States must work to build up a powerful middle-of-the road regime in China. But Washington continued to back Chiang Kai-shek and pour millions of dollars into his coffers.

The Japanese Consulate in Java. A centre of espionage where Japan plotted Java's downfall before World War II

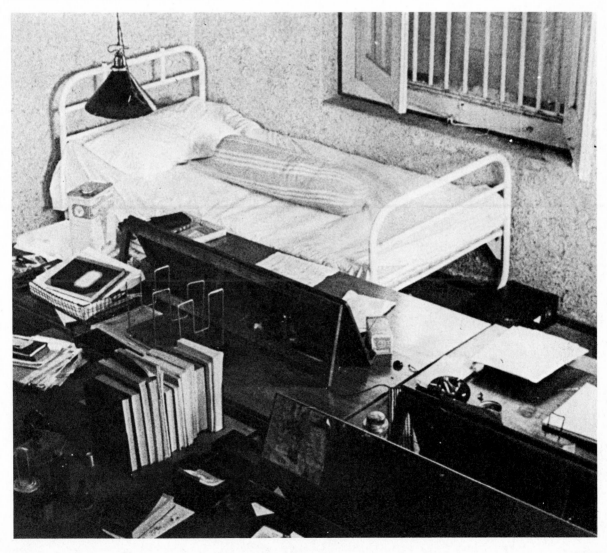

'. . and here is an enlargement of your microfilm survey of "important installations" in the Urals'

After World War II the Central Intelligence Agency became the global espionage service of the United States and began to supersede some of the lesser rival Intelligence agencies. It developed and expanded during and as a result of the 'Cold War', the state of uneasy peace amounting at times almost to undeclared war which existed in the immediate post-war years between the Western Allies and the Soviet Union.

As one Russian spy after another was unmasked inside the United States and in Britain and France it swiftly became apparent that all the time the USA and Russia had been allies during the war, the espionage services of the Soviet Union had been conducting a massive campaign inside Allied territories.

The 'Cold War' was largely fought out by the spy services of the two super-powers, the United States and the Soviet Union. While the FBI uncovered a whole series of Russian spy networks inside the USA, most of them designed to discover America's nuclear secrets and the development of atomic weapons, the CIA sought to build up inside Europe an army of agents to ascertain Russian plans of aggression.

At first the successes scored were mainly by the USA's counter-espionage – the FBI. Under J Edgar Hoover's direction the FBI not only broke up Russian spy networks in America, but unmasked similar networks in Britain and France. It was the FBI who paved the way to the arrest of Klaus Fuchs, the atomic spy operating in Britain, and first warned the British of the existence of traitors inside the British Foreign Office and Secret Service in the persons of Donald Maclean, Guy Burgess and 'Kim' Philby.

Had Britain acted more promptly on repeated warnings from FBI sources, all these men could have been caught. In the end each one of them escaped to Soviet Russia.

After any major war the first redundancies of personnel occur in the Secret Services of the powers concerned and

Dr Klaus Fuchs. Imprisoned for 9 years in Great Britain for betraying Atomic Secrets

many secret agents find themselves without employment. But the 'Cold War' prevented this from happening after World War II. Indeed, the United States found that its need for more agents was so acute that personnel had to be sought among other nationals.

Though criticised by many for what seemed to be making friends with the enemy with indecent haste, the CIA decided, with Government support, that, with the Soviet Union showing hostility to America, it was a wise policy to make friends with Germany rather than see her drift towards an alliance with Russia again.

Under Stalin's ruthless rule of terror it had been almost impossible to plant American spies in Russia with the same ease that the Soviet Union had been able to create spy networks in the USA. The CIA argued that the only nation which had a nucleus of spies in Russia in sufficient numbers to obtain intelligence was the defeated enemy, Germany, who during the invasion of Russia by the Wehrmacht, had made contact with anti-Communist Russians.

The CIA had a bonus in the person of General Reinhard Gehlen. Having become Hitler's chief of intelligence on the Eastern Front and, so it is said, infiltrated spies into Stalin's War Council, Gehlen organised all German intelligence in Russia and the Balkans in World War II. At the end of the war, having first taken the precaution of hiding all his archives in the mountains of Bavaria, he suddenly delivered himself and his Intelligence service to the Americans.

As a result there developed the Gehlen Organisation, backed by the CIA a service which aimed at being supreme in obtaining intelligence on Soviet Russia. It paved the way for Gehlen being accepted as an ally of the West.

As a prisoner-of-war in 1945 Gehlen made a deal with the Americans and so impressed them that the Gehlen

**General Reinhard Gehlen.
Director of West German
Intelligence**

Organisation was financed by the CIA to the extent of 600 million dollars.

This is perhaps the first instance in history of one Secret Service using the Intelligence chief of an enemy nation for its own ends and finally paving the way for that man to re-organise the former enemy's Secret Service. For ultimately Gehlen became chief of the West German Intelligence Service.

In the 'fifties Gehlen was the CIA's main instrument in fighting the 'Cold War' inside Russia and East Germany, by then a Communist satellite state. For a while Gehlen was probably the most powerful Secret Service chief in Europe, encouraged by the Americans, mistrusted by the British and French, the ex-Nazi who had made good.

Two of Gehlen's top agents

Gehlen already had a small network of spies inside Russia and East Germany. When the CIA increased his budget he set about infiltrating Russia and East Germany with his own agents. Thus he was able for a few years to keep the Americans closely informed on developments inside these territories. In addition he helped to organise the Berlin Rising in 1953 and the Hungarian Revolt of 1956, as well as organising Nasser's Secret Service in Egypt and then infiltrating an Israeli spy into that country.

By 1955 Gehlen had become head of Western German Intelligence, though he still helped the Americans. But he had made the fatal mistake of over-infiltrating Russia with his agents, and East Germany, too. The Russians quickly realised what Gehlen was up to and, instead of closing in and making mass arrests, they just let the agents settle down, kept a watch on them and then systematically turned the tables by infiltrating their own agents into Gehlen's ranks.

The Soviet Intelligence slowly but surely 'took over' several key men in the Gehlen Organisation. By 1962-3 the effects of this were being felt. Not only was the Soviet Union gaining a foothold in Gehlen's camp, but even managing to infiltrate the CIA. The full story of this espionage failure has not only yet to be told, but its effects are still reverberating down the corridors of Eastern and Middle Europe.

'Toni', whose recruitment as an agent was described in chapter one, believes that gadgetry and technical know-how have enabled the CIA to keep pace with the Russians in the espionage war.

For a time 'Toni' operated a radio-receiver on a Taiwan mountain summit and learned about the spying done by the US SR-71 (SR for Strategic Reconnaisance).

'Our global espionage today is greatly boosted by the spy-planes and multi-purpose Project 647 surveillance satellites which buzz and bleep around the world, providing the photographic and radar-obtained data which give us a picture of what goes on in the Communist world,' 'Toni' told me.

'When spy-planes became too embarrassing after the U-2 affair we began to rely on the satellites which are equipped with black-and-white, colour and TV cameras. They can sweep the whole of Russia and Asia.

'If Russia or China should make secret atomic blasts, our satellite equipment and cameras can record them.'

At the National Security Headquarters at Fort Meade the results of these aerial probes are recorded in a gigantic bank of computers which absorbs a vast amount of intelligence and also helps to tackle the ever-present problem of code-breaking.

'At one time I used to think that perhaps we obtained too much information, that eventually we shouldn't be able to

Ariel photograph showing missile launch stands in Cuba

tell what was valuable and vital and what was useless and irrelevant. But once you get a desk job you begin to change your mind.

'I had a desk job for six months once. My task was to read reports coming from overseas and to analyse them. I soon found that I needed to ask for all kinds of additional data from our files in order to check these reports.

'You see, unless you really do your homework – and that means reading through masses of background information – you can't possibly interrogate another agent properly. De-briefing is what we call it in the Service. To de-brief you have to let the man you are questioning know you are aware of what has been going on in Berlin, Warsaw and a host of other places.

'This is particularly important when interrogating defectors. There is always a small percentage of defectors who are

Steve's restaurant near Waterloo Station, London, where Lonsdale and Houghton met to pass information

infiltrated agents. You have to try to spot them. Once you have caught them out in a lie, or at least some item of false information, you have to prepare the ground for someone else to question them when you have finished.

'A lie doesn't necessarily mean a defector is an enemy agent. But it puts you on your guard. He could have been told lies and accepted them unwittingly.

'Another job I had at this time was to find suitable sites for leaving messages and arranging meeting places for agents. This meant not only looking up large-scale maps of such cities as Warsaw, Budapest and Prague, but obtaining photographs to find easily recognisable trees, bridges, park benches and other clearly definable meeting places which could be pin-pointed without error. All this required much more thought than one would imagine. A slight error on my part and an agent's cover might have been broken.'

'Toni' believed that 'Operation Gold' was one of the great successes of the CIA in the 'fifties. This was the operation in which a tunnel was built from West Berlin to East Berlin so that the CIA could tap Russian and East German telephones. Started in 1953, the tunnel was extended and messages regularly tapped without interruption until in 1956 it was discovered by the Russians.

The tunnel started in a suburb of Rudow, near a cemetery, and ran for about half a mile under the barbed wire fences of the border into Alt Glienicke in East Berlin. It was in effect an example of close co-operation between the CIA and the British Secret Service.

'Toni' tells this story about the tunnel:

'The idea came from one of our CIA communications experts who happened to discover that the main trunk telephone cables between East Berlin and Leipzig passed underground only about 350 yards from the American sector

The US radar station built to conceal the Berlin Tunnel

of Berlin. By his knowledge of communications routes he deducted that these cables would carry messages from the East German Army HQ.

'Many questions needed to be answered before we could get the necessary details to enable us to tap the lines. This is why we pooled our resources with the British. When we were actually starting the tunnel we had grave doubts as to whether the ploughed field above us would cave in and give the whole game away. However, we finished the job and tape recorders were plugged into the telephone lines and operated day and night for several months.

'Eventually the scouts we employed to watch the road above the tunnel saw a Russian telephone repair team arrive and start digging. We knew then that discovery was imminent and we just had time to evacuate our people from the tunnel back into the American zone.'

The Berlin Tunnel

The CIA became the eyes and ears of the Western World in Berlin in this period. Yet after Richard Helms became chief of the CIA America's espionage system came under greater criticism than ever before. At first this came only from foreign countries. Then the CIA came under fire in the United States, from newspapers, Senators and Congressmen, and even from President Kennedy himself.

The gist of the complaints was that the CIA threatened to become bigger than America itself, that it was almost dictating US foreign policy. Suddenly the spotlight was on the big, grey building overlooking the Potonac River as it gently wound its way through Virginia, the home set in 140 secluded acres which was the headquarters of the CIA.

It was alleged that the CIA had wielded unlimited powers for fourteen years, helping to overthrow governments in small countries, in some cases infiltrating and controlling foreign trade unions, organising coups and kidnappings.

Matters came to a head with the disastrous Bay of Pigs attempted invasion of Cuba in 1961 after which an enraged President, putting all the blame on the CIA, threatened that he would 'splinter' it 'into a thousand pieces and scatter it to the winds'.

No leader in modern times had spoken so harshly of his Secret Service, but the CIA survived this outburst, though its powers were drastically clipped thereafter.

Of course, the difficulty always is to keep a balance between paying due heed to a Secret Service and giving it a certain amount of freedom of action and not controlling it sufficiently. As we have seen in the case of China in World War II, the Government was wrong and the Secret Service was right. Perhaps the reverse was true with the Bay of Pigs and again when CIA chief Richard Helms tipped off journalists that Russia was considering making a pre-emptive air strike against

The CIA Headquarters

Missile Equipment loaded in Cuba

Kruschev and Kennedy

nuclear installations in China. On that occasion Mr William Rogers, of the State Department, issued a furious denial of Helms' claim.

Yet the fact remains the CIA has played a vital role in helping to contain and frustrate Russian aggression in many areas of the world. Without its help and initiative the world situation might be very much worse today. If Americans can sleep relatively safely without fear of surprise nuclear attack, this is as much due to the CIA, the FBI, the National Security Agency in Maryland with its electronic devices and code-breaking and the Defence Intelligence Agency which co-ordinates intelligence reports from the Army and Navy, as to any other single factor.

Chapter 5

Great spies of history

As spying becomes more sophisticated so the feats of individual spies make more fascinating reading, though the probability is that we are very close to witnessing the end of the era of the great individual spy. Team work, the assessing of reports from several agents and even the advent of the computer have all tended to create less scope for the single agent.

Nevertheless history has shown that one man alone can sometimes achieve as much as a whole army in positive espionage achievements and to place too much emphasis on team work could very easily frustrate and destroy the work of the brilliant individual spy. Espionage is very often a matter of intuition plus experience, something the single skilled agent can possess, but not an army of spies.

The qualities that go to make a great spy are almost indefinable and in any case they vary from one individual to another. Some, like Sidney Reilly, reveal their genius in sheer power of personality; others, like Richard Sorge, depend on sheer determination and the ability to be a loner over long periods, while with Jules Silber the outstanding quality was self-descipline allied to extreme caution. What these men had in common was enormous strength of character and will-power.

Legend has made the name of Mata Hari symbolic of the super-spy and of feminine intrigue. Alas, it was not like that at all. Her real name was much less glamorous – Margaret Gertrude Macleod – and her brief career as a spy was inept, unskilled and totally undistinguished. But for her exotic beauty and the fact that she was caught and shot she would long since have been forgotten.

Born in Holland, she was the child of stolid Dutch parents. As a young girl she was married to a captain in the Dutch colonial forces in Java and his brutal treatment of her may well

Mata Hari, photographed in Paris in 1905

have been the cause of her deliberate decision to exploit the weaknesses of men in order to obtain and sell information. In Java she became passionately interested in the dances of that country and she studied and practised them so effectively that eventually she was able to pose as Mata Hari, the Javanese dancer.

It was in this role that she became known in Paris, Berlin and other European capitals, having finally escaped from the clutches of her brutal and drunken Dutch husband, who was of Scottish extraction. Perhaps his links with Britain made her anti-British. At any rate, long before 1914, she was passing information to the Germans, having become the mistress of a number of German Army officers. Perhaps they flattered her into believing she could become a spy.

Probably Mata Hari made more money from her dancing and from her many male admirers than she did from espionage. She was indiscreet, she flaunted her friendships with the 'enemy' so that long before World War I was declared the French Secret Service knew she was in the pay of the Germans.

Mata Hari in one of her famous Eastern Dances

But her sense of being a *femme fatale*, of having power and influence over men in important positions, went to her head. Her first major blunder was offering her services to Captain Georges Ladoux of the *Deuxième Bureau*, the French counter-espionage service.

Ladoux pretended to trust her and gave her the names of various agents in Belgium, all of whom were of doubtful reliability. This way, so Ladoux thought, he could at least put the agents to the test.

One of them was arrested by the Germans and shot. The French had always suspected that he was a double agent as he had never given them any worthwhile information. They checked with the British who confirmed that he had also worked for them, but that he had been betrayed to the Germans by a woman. Everything pointed to Mata Hari having revealed the agent's name to the Germans.

Shortly afterwards Mata Hari came to England where she was promptly interviewed by Sir Basil Thomson, head of the Special Branch of Scotland Yard. Sir Basil had a habit of putting suspects he interviewed in a very low seat close to his desk so that he could look down on them. She told him that she was indeed a spy, but for the French, not the Germans. Sir Basil, who was even then convinced of her guilt, warned her to give up espionage or it would land her in trouble. It was a courteous warning and today it would have been sufficient to force any spy to lie low for a while. Mata Hari paid no heed: she was allowed to leave England for neutral Spain where she immediately contacted the German naval attaché.

From that point on, with the Secret Services of Britain

and France on her tail, Mata Hari was doomed. When she returned to France, the French promptly arrested her. She was tried, evidence was given of her having received money from German Secret Service funds and passing "information" *of what?* to the enemy, and finally she was sentenced to death.

She died bravely at the hands of the firing squad, her bravado and sense of dignity preserved to the last. Thus her death was the beginning of a legend and the phrase 'a Mata Hari' became synonymous in the next generation with a description of a beautiful and heroic spy. Thirty-five years later history repeated itself. In 1952 it was reported that Mata Hari's daughter, Banda Gertrud, had been shot as a spy in Korea.

Events took an ironic twist for whereas her mother had been shot as an enemy of Britain and of France, her daughter was executed because she worked on behalf of Britain. Banda

Another Mother and Daughter Spy team. As they normally appeared and in disguise

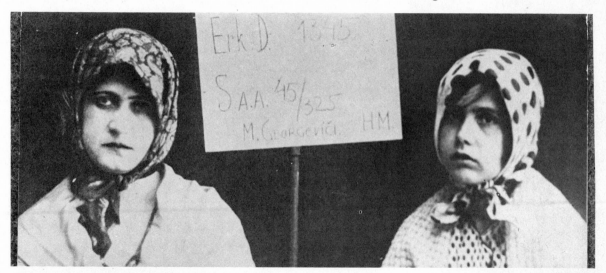

was only seventeen years of age when, living with relatives in Batavia, she learned that her mother had been executed as a spy. She changed her name and it was not for another thirty years that the Intelligence Services of Britain and the USA learned her true identity.

Banda was attractive like her mother, but clever as well. She went to college and became a teacher and might well have remained one but for the invasion of the Dutch East Indies by the Japanese in World War II. Then she learned that, like her mother before her, she had to become a spy. But, unlike her mother, she did not stoop to low and sordid intrigues. She merely listened to the Japanese who came to her parties and passed on information to the Indonesian underground and the Allies.

As one who looked upon herself as a Eurasian, Banda wanted to help the native peoples of the Far East. After the war she met and fell in love with a Malaysian guerrilla who believed that the best way of gaining independence for his country was by supporting the Malaysian Chinese Communists. Banda persuaded him that he was wrong and together they worked against the guerrillas and bandits of Malaya and passed information to the British.

Banda went to Washington and was able to convince important people there that the Malayan War was not just a question of Britain keeping down the natives and that the quickest way for independence to be achieved by the Malaysian people as a whole was by supporting the British. By this time she had good reason to back the British cause: her husband had been murdered by the Communists.

Her doom was sealed when she was sent on a secret mission to Korea as a spy. Ultimately she was discovered by the Communists and shot. History had repeated itself.

One of the most remarkable spies of all time was Sidney Reilly, alias Sigmund Georgievich Rosenblum, son of a Polish-Jewish landowner from Warsaw.

It is a curiously recurring feature in stories about ace spies that the best of them very often come from complex and diverse backgrounds and mixed nationality. I do not think any moral can be drawn from this, but it is obvious that someone who has cosmopolitan origins with perhaps divided loyalties may perhaps become a more objective spy than one whose roots are only in a single country. He acquires the gift for seeing situations from all angles.

Sidney Reilly was certainly a double, probably a treble and possibly a quadruple agent. The full extent of his espionage activities has not yet been established. He even kept the secret of his true origins for many years, something which any spy today would find hard to do—at least as far as his employers were concerned.

Sidney Reilly

Born on 24 March, 1874, he seems to have been an unhappy child, anxious to leave home as soon as possible. He ran away from his family while still in his teens, stowing away on a British ship bound for South America. When he arrived there he had a variety of jobs, as docker, road-mender and plantation worker. Then he had a lucky break: he got the job of cook to a British expeditionary party in Brazil, the leader of which, a Major Fothergill, happened to be a member of the British Secret Service.

This was Reilly's first real chance and he was determined to make the most of it. Not only did he prove to be a good cook, but, when the expedition lost their way, it was he who guided them to safety. When attacked by natives it was Reilly again who showed amazing marksmanship by picking them off one by one. It was as a result of his initiative and zealous service on the expedition that he was given a paid passage to Britain and an introduction to a high-up member of the Secret Service.

That was about 1896 and for the next thirty years Reilly was engaged in espionage, something of an all-time record in a profession which is not noted for longevity of service. Few last the pace for such an incredible time.

He was first sent to Russia and one must assume that he did good work here because in his early years in the Secret Service Reilly sometimes displayed a devil-may-care approach to his job. He married a wealthy young English widow and then disappeared completely for a year. Most agents on probation in the early part of their careers would have got the sack for less, but Reilly's previous good work for the Service allied to his breath-taking impudence seem to have persuaded the authorities to give him another chance.

His audacity of approach is not to be recommended as a model for other spies, but it bears the hall-mark of the cosmopolitan genius:

'By acquiring a British wife,' Sidney nonchalantly told his senior officers, 'I am giving myself closer links with Britain and taking root in the country which employs me. But, more important from your point of view, my wife has money which enables me to have the necessary cash to be able to afford to work for the Secret Service. Otherwise I fear I could not afford to serve an organisation which pays me so badly. I have also now given myself the name of Sidney Reilly which in effect makes me British. But it is also the name of an Irishman, and I have given myself an Irish birthplace so that, if necessary in the course of my future work, I can pose as being anti-British by making myself out to be an Irish Nationalist!'

What can one reply to a man like this? You can dismiss him as an erratic eccentric, or you can take a gamble that his eccentricity and bravado will pay off. Years later at a British Consulate on the Continent an official queried Reilly's passport. 'At lunch you were telling us that you were born in Odessa,' he said to Reilly. 'How comes it that on your passport you are entered as "Sidney George Reilly, born in Tipperary"?'

'There was a war on and I came to fight for England,' replied Reilly unabashed. 'I needed a British passport and therefore a British birthplace, and you see, from Odessa, it's a long, long way to Tipperary.'

Even when giving this explanation Reilly was not telling the whole truth. It is correct that in World War I, when he was in Canada and wanted to join the Royal Flying Corps, he needed a British passport. But by then he had already been in possession of one for several years.

Shortly before the Russo-Japanese War, Reilly turned up in the Far East as a double-agent serving both the British and

A Press cutting of his wedding

ACTRESS'S WEDDING.

FROM NURSING HOME TO REGISTER OFFICE.

Mrs. Haddon Chambers, well known under her stage name of Pepita Bobadilla, was well enough to leave the nursing home to-day for her wedding to Captain Sidney George Reilly, at the Register Office, Henrietta-street, W.C.

Mrs. Chambers looked charming in a black tailor-made costume, with an ermine stole and a

THE BRIDE AND BRIDEGROOM.
(Photographed to-day.)

small red hat. She carried a bouquet of lilies of the valley.

The bride and bridegroom were accompanied by Mrs. Alice Menzies, the bride's sister, Capt. George Alexander Hill, D.S.O., and Major Stephen Alley, M.C., all of whom signed the register.

Comrades in Arms.

Capt. Hill and Capt. Reilly were formerly in the R.A.F., and had many thrilling adventures in Russia and the Baltic provinces.

It was on Wednesday that Reilly asked Capt. Hill to stand by him at the wedding to-day as he had stood by him during the war.

The ceremony was a quiet one, and no reception was held on account of the bride's health. The honeymoon will be spent on the Continent.

the Japanese. Again he sent in some excellent reports to the British, warning them of the imminence of war. But he must have perplexed his Secret Service chief in London once again when he asked for a year's absence of leave on the grounds that he did not want to do anything which might impair his relations with the Russians.

Surprisingly, his request was granted and Reilly went off to China where for several months he lived in a lamasery and became a Buddhist. Then he returned to Russia and, while still working for the British, is rumoured to have started spying for the Russians. It may well be that at this time he was making more money out of the Russians as in 1906 he had a lavish apartment in St Petersburg, had acquired a splendid art collection and was a member of the most exclusive club in the city.

Of course, at this time Britain and Russia, then under Czarist rule, were allies so that if he had been working for the Russians as well, this did not mean he was betraying the British. But he had almost certainly double-crossed the Japanese to whom he had previously sold information about Russia.

Capt Sir Mansfield Cumming, who was head of the British Secret Service at that time, said of Reilly: 'By the time I joined the SIS Reilly was not only an agent of long standing, but he had almost made himself indispensable. He had guts and genius, but he was too much of a politician, the last thing a good agent should be.'

Reilly always took the law into his own hands and frequently acted on his own initiative. For example, while working as a welder in Krupp's arms works in Germany before World War I, he not only stole the plans of the arms factory, but killed two watchmen in making his getaway. Then he got the job as sole agent in Russia for a firm of German naval ship-builders. By this means he managed to see and to copy all blueprints, plans and specifications of the latest German naval construction. These he passed back to Britain.

But it was a highly dangerous game for him to play. The Germans did not know he was a British agent, but they were sufficiently suspicious to have him watched day and night. However his method of disarming German suspicions was to let the British colony in St Petersburg know that he was taking large sums in commissions from the Germans for winning orders for the Russians for ship-building which might so easily have gone to a British firm.

The Germans learned that the British colony in St Petersburg was more suspicious of Reilly than they were themselves and that they were not only ostracising him, but demanding that he should be sent home. Reilly also had the impudence to point out to the British Secret Service that by taking commissions from the Germans he was patriotically saving the British the cost of paying him a proper salary.

At the beginning of World War I Reilly was in the Far East again. Then he went to the United States and bought arms supplies for the Russians. There are grounds for believing that at this time he may have been helping the American Secret Service as well. But in 1917 he arrived back in Britain, joined the Royal Flying Corps and was parachuted behind the German lines on a number of occasions. Once, disguised as a German, he spent three weeks inside Germany, gathering information about the next planned thrust against the Allies. For all these missions he was decorated with the Military Cross.

But Reilly's greatest feats were those which crowned his career after World War I. This was the period of the Bolshevik revolution and the attempts by some of the Allied powers to put an end to communist rule in that country by supporting a counter-revolution. The trouble was that the governments of the Allied countries were mostly in disagreement on the subject. Some wanted to intervene actively with armed forces against the Bolsheviks, others preferred to remain neutral while a few, including Britain, wanted to compromise by using Secret Service intrigues to bring about the downfall of the Communists.

Sidney Reilly was recognised as the most experienced agent Britain had regarding Russian affairs. In April, 1918, it was decided to send him to Russia, partly as a secret agent, but, dangerously, also as an unofficial envoy of the British Government. This was a risky business in two ways: it made the Bolsheviks aware of his presence in Russia and it gave Reilly the chance to play his own game as a policy-maker. In retrospect it was a classic blunder for espionage and politics do not mix.

The Bolsheviks became so suspicious of Reilly that he was forced to go underground: they did not believe his cover story that he had come out specially to make a personal report for the British Prime Minister, Lloyd George, because the British did not trust the reports they had had from diplomats on the spot. Indeed, it is doubtful if Lloyd George would have approved of this cover story.

Disguising himself as a Turkish merchant, Reilly began to plot not only with the counter-revolutionaries, but some of the more moderate revolutionaries. Perhaps power had gone to his head and he saw himself as a politician, saving Russia from communist terror and creating his own government in place of the Bolsheviks.

He raised funds for a counter-revolutionary coup and began to form his own shadow cabinet, while working out a scheme for having all the Red leaders arrested at a meeting which was to be held in August, 1918. If the plot had succeeded, Sidney

Reilly might have changed the course of history. But all was ruined when a woman tried to assassinate Lenin and the Bolsheviks ordered the arrest of a large number of suspects as a result of which Reilly's plot was uncovered.

During the next few years Reilly made frequent trips in and out of Russia, sometimes even carrying around with him a pass showing him to be a member of the Cheka, the dreaded Russian secret police. In the late 1920's there emerged a strange secret organisation known as 'The Trust', apparently backed by anti-Bolshevik Russians in exile in Finland and the United States and supposedly with backing inside Russia from counter-revolutionaries. Reilly told the British Secret Service that he believed in the authenticity of 'The Trust' and suggested he should make one further trip to Russia.

In September, 1925, he made his last, fatal mission to Russia. News came through that he had been shot while trying to cross the border from Finland. After that there was a long silence. Various reports came back to London from individuals who claimed either to have seen Reilly alive, or to have heard that he was in prison in Russia. But there was nothing conclusive.

The mystery of Reilly's death

Finally 'The Trust' was revealed as a bogus organisation, purporting to support counter-revolutionaries and trying to lure them back to Russia, but actually controlled by the Russian Secret Service. It is hard to see how so shrewd and experienced a character as Reilly could have been deceived in this way.

Thereby lies a mystery which has not been unravelled to this day. There are three possibilities: that Reilly was fooled by the Russians, that he went back to Russia to turn against his former employers, or that, with a sublime belief in his own genius, he was under no illusions about 'The Trust', but that he thought he could pretend to join the Bolsheviks and actually double-cross them in the long run.

Personally, I subscribe to the last theory. The Russians in their own journal, *Nedelya*, in June, 1966, have given their own version of the fate of Sidney Reilly. They admit that he was lured back into Russia by 'The Trust', but claim that he was not shot at the border, but captured and held in custody. The article stated that on 13 October, 1925, Reilly wrote to Dzershinsky, head of the Cheka, saying that he was ready to co-operate with the Soviet and to give them full information on the British and American Intelligence agencies. According to *Nedelya* Reilly was executed on 5 November, 1925. Other reports suggest he was still alive in 1927.

An undoubted rogue, a brilliant agent, a brave man and still an enigma: that just about sums up Sidney Reilly.

From glamorous, luxury-loving Sidney Reilly, with his zest for gay parties, lots of girl friends and an impish delight in having a finger in every political pie, we come to a very different type of 'ace' spy – Jules Crawford Silber, one of the ablest agents Germany ever put into the field.

Silber was the model of the quiet, unostentatious, cautious operator who bides his time until the big moment arrives, content with a humdrum role, but all the time preparing himself to achieve greatness at the right moment.

The Germans have had many brave spies, but most of them have been singularly unlucky. Perhaps their bravery has sometimes been their undoing, but the chief weakness of German espionage over the years has been a tendency to follow the rules too rigidly. Discipline, a regard for the elementary rules of espionage, these things are all important, but in the spy game the sudden emergency, the unexpected incident, calls for initiative rather than the rule book. It is in this that so often they have fallen down just as the reverse was true in the case of Sidney Reilly: his penchant for going it alone was his downfall.

Jules Silber left Germany in the mid-1880's, settling in South America where he perfected his English and was in fact commended for his services to Britain during the Boer War. This commendation was to prove invaluable to him when war broke out in 1914. He was then in the United States and he decided there and then that his patriotic duty was to serve his country.

Maybe Silber had decided on a career as a spy before he helped the British in the Boer War. Possibly he was even then gathering intelligence for Germany in a small way. He first went to Canada and, after showing his certificate of commendation from the British, managed to obtain a set of Canadian identity papers, armed with which he travelled to London.

There his credentials were accepted and, on the strength of his knowledge of languages, he was given a job in the Postal Censorship Department. Sober, industrious, naturally a man of integrity and extremely conscientious in his duties, he soon became an admirable member of the censorship team. He also made friends very easily.

Part of his job was to check correspondence passing through the censorship and to compare addresses on the envelopes with those on an official list of suspected German 'post boxes' in neutral Holland through which intelligence reports might be forwarded. To any such letters he was instructed by the British to pay the closest attention.

Now Silber was not formally engaged as a German agent, at least at this stage. He had never received any training in espionage. But certainly while he had been in America, and probably as long ago as his stay in South Africa, he had communicated with the German authorities and offered to help in any way he could. Thus at this stage he was largely a self-employed agent working for Germany.

But he learned quickly and he took few risks. Wisely he continued as a 'loner' and made no attempt to contact other German agents or officials in Britain. His job in the censor's office gave him unique opportunities for getting in touch with his own people.

It was the British themselves who really presented Silber with the ideal opportunity for spying. Throughout the war he posted on secrets in envelopes which bore his official stamp, 'Passed by Censor' without arousing any hint of suspicion.

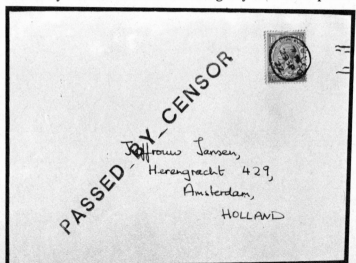

The letter to Holland

Each one of these letters was sent on to one or other of the suspected enemy 'post boxes' on the official list which was, of course, revised from time to time. From Holland the letters were speedily passed to Germany.

Later, when he was transferred to Liverpool, he operated through addresses in the USA, sometimes putting into a parcel addressed to a New York bank a letter in a plain envelope with 'Please forward' marked on it. The bank were naturally not suspicious in view of the fact that the parcel had been passed by the censor.

While other German spies sent to Britain were usually rounded up within a matter of months, if not weeks, Silber went from strength to strength. He began to acquire tit-bits of information himself as well as being able to slip through other agents' messages. Much of the information he passed on he acquired from material that was actually banned by the censor's department.

A study of Silber's methods will show how important patience and attention to small details are to enable a spy to survive. Mainly he relied on his memory for passing on information, going back to his lodgings and carefully informing the people there that he was going to a theatre, then slipping off to a secret address where he committed to paper all he could remember. Sometimes he took documents and letters away with him and photographed them himself, returning them to the censorship office next day.

All this work was invaluable espionage to the Germans, but nearly all of it was dull, plodding routine. Then at last Silber showed that when a lucky chance came his way this stolid, desk-bound censor could act with something of the panache of a Sidney Reilly.

While going through the correspondence Silber noticed a letter from a young woman, living near Devonport dockyard, in which she said how delighted she was that her brother, a naval officer, had got a shore job near where she was living. 'It's something to do with refitting an old ship. He doesn't say very much, but, as you know, he is a gunnery officer.'

Silber pondered on those words. It looked as though the officer might be engaged in some hush-hush work and that his sister was hinting at such. He read on and learned that the old ship was a merchantman. What would the Royal Navy be doing with a merchantman and how did a gunnery officer come to be involved in all this?

Acting on the hunch that he was on the verge of making an important discovery, Silber told the man in charge of the censor's office that he did not feel well and would like to take the afternoon off. His request was granted and within a short time he was on a train bound for Plymouth.

Having got the young woman's address, he had no difficulty in locating her quickly. Showing her the letter she had written,

A 'Q' Boat

he inquired whether she realised that not only had she committed an offence by writing about such matters, but that there was a real risk that her brother could be sent to prison for a breach of the Official Secrets Act.

'How much has your brother told you?' he asked.

Now desperately frightened, even more for her brother than for herself, the girl told Silber everything: how this merchantman and others like it were to be secretly armed with hidden guns and manned by Royal Naval crews. The German spy had stumbled across his most sensational coup of the war, the discovery of the innovation of Q-boats, which were deliberately to lure German submarines to their doom.

Prior to this when German submarines encountered ships sailing alone, the crews were normally ordered to take to the boats before the ships were sunk by gun-fire. With the Q-boats the plan was for half a Q-boat's crew to lower the boats, when challenged, but as soon as the submarine closed to point-blank range in readiness to sink the ship the remaining crew would throw open the hatches which concealed their guns, open fire and sink the submarine.

Silber thanked the young woman for being so frank with him, said he was prepared to overlook the offence, if she promised never to repeat it and also to keep his visit to her secret from anyone, including her brother. It was his duty to take action against both of them, but he did not wish to see a young officer's career ruined and for this reason he was taking a risk.

There is little doubt that the frightened girl was easily silenced and Silber returned to London and sent off his message about the Q-boats in an envelope stamped with 'passed by censor.'

The Germans reacted swiftly. From then on no merchant-

Troops in World War I

men were given a chance to take to their boats by German submarines: they were sunk by torpedo without warning.

And Silber's future? In due course, when the war was over, he returned to Germany, having successfully evaded detection for four years. The British had no idea of the existence of this spy in their midst until in 1932 he wrote a book telling the whole story.

One of the assets of the 'ace' spy who wishes to survive should be a capacity for seeming to be just an ordinary, good fellow – 'a regular guy'. One such was Richard Sorge.

An intelligence officer who knew him well, but still never suspected his identity, told me: 'Sorge was the last man you would expect to be a spy. He was gregarious, friendly, relaxed and a very ordinary type of chap, never appearing to be curious about anything except eating, drinking and pretty girls.'

Yet Richard Sorge was probably the ablest spy Soviet Russia ever put into the field. After his death the Russians made him the coveted award of Hero of the Soviet Union and the official commentator of *Pravda* wrote of him that he was 'a man whose name will become the symbol of devotion to the great cause of the fight for peace, the symbol of courage and heroism'.

And, if independent and objective confirmation of that assessment is required, it is supplied by the American General Douglas MacArthur, who said that Sorge's story represented 'a devastating example of a brilliant success in espionage – its evolution, techniques and methods'.

Sorge was born in Baku in Southern Russia in 1895, the son of a German engineer and a Russian woman. During World War I he served in the German Army as a private. Surprisingly, for one of his ability and initiative, he does not seem to have gained any promotion, but this may be due to the fact that he was twice wounded and indeed on the first occasion he was actually discharged from the Army and had great difficulty in enlisting again.

After the war he went to university in Germany, took a doctorate in political science and then, after spells of work as a teacher, coal miner and journalist, became a member of the German Communist Party in 1922.

Richard Sorge. Leader of a Soviet Spy Ring in Japan

The fact that he spoke Russian and German fluently and like a native, as well as speaking other languages tolerably well, was noted by agents of the Soviet Intelligence. In 1925 he was recruited into the GRU section of the Russian Secret Service, a body mainly concerned with military espionage overseas.

Unlike either Reilly or Silber, Sorge was properly trained as a spy. He underwent a long course in espionage at one of the crack spy schools in Russia. Not until 1927 did he get his first assignment.

The Russians are careful when they send newly fledged agents into action and usually give them a dummy run in obtaining relatively easy and innocuous 'intelligence', and in this respect Sorge was no exception. The task he was given must have been a pleasant one: it was simply to go to Los Angeles and make a report on the Hollywood film industry! His cover was that of a German journalist.

For the next few years Sorge worked in Britain, Scandinavia and the Balkans. No doubt the Russians were still somewhat on their guard about employing a man who had a German father at a time when Germany was the sworn enemy of Russia. But eventually they seemed satisfied with his progress and he was transferred to the Fourth Bureau of the Red Army General Staff and told to form an espionage network in the Far East.

Sorge undertook his task with enthusiasm, drive and much resourcefulness. He recruited agents in Canton, Nanking, Hanchow, Peking, Tokyo and Yokohama and at the same time set about learning and mastering the Chinese and Japanese languages. Indeed, he was so thorough in his desire to learn all he could about the countries to which he had been sent that he studied their literature and their political systems. Though a natural play-boy, his iron self-discipline enabled him to spend long hours at his books.

Sorge's talent for picking sound and loyal agents was remarkable. Perhaps to ensure their loyalty to him personally he chose mainly from Americans, Chinese, Germans and Japanese, always taking care to select those with pro-Soviet views. With very few exceptions he avoided Russians.

His reports revealed not merely a wealth of detail, but shrewd and prophetic analyses of what he saw and heard. Earlier Soviet agents in Japan had optimistically forecast that Japan posed no serious threat to the USSR. Sorge warned that Russia was faced by the possibility of a German–Japanese alliance which would threaten her on her western and eastern borders at the same time. Because of this he concentrated his espionage network on Japan.

Then he submitted to the Russians a plan so audacious that it had to be approved by Stalin himself. This was that he should go to Germany, make contact with leading Nazis and join the Nazi Party.

The risks of such a plan were enormous. Though his father had been of German nationality, Sorge had a police dossier on him dating back to his student days and his membership of the German Communist Party. To apply to join the Nazi Party generally meant a waiting period while the credentials of the would-be member were checked. Had his past record come to light he would undoubtedly have been imprisoned summarily and probably sentenced to death.

Sorge, however, possessed great charm and it is probable that his self-assured talk, his offer to spy for the Germans and the close relations he had established with leading Nazis caused the authorities not to look too closely into his antecedents. He was not only accepted into the Party, but returned to Tokyo as the correspondent of a German newspaper.

Once installed in Tokyo, Sorge's double game began to pay off. He made close friends with Lieutenant-Colonel Eugen Ott, who was attached to the Japanese Army as a liaison officer, and more or less had the freedom of the German Embassy. Soon he was passing back to Moscow copies of secret reports which the Germans were sending to Berlin. Sometimes he photographed documents in the Embassy with his miniature pocket camera.

In a short while Sorge was feeding the Germans with information he gleaned from the Japanese and the Russians with material he obtained from Japanese and German sources. This covered a wide range from intelligence and operational reports from Manchuria to the battle order of the Japanese army and air force and joint German – Japanese policy towards Russia.

All this activity on his part required great concentration and self-composure, not to mention strong nerves. He not only had to be on his guard with the Germans and to pose as a staunch Nazi supporter, but to contend with a day and night watch kept on him by the Japanese secret police. He knew that the latter questioned his servants about his movements. Sorge's method of putting them off the scent was to give the impression that he spent his spare time in giving wild parties and entertaining girls.

The most valuable information he gave the Russians – and this may well have saved them from defeat in 1941-2 – was that Germany was planning to invade Russia in the spring of 1941 and that the Japanese, believing the Germans would win, were transferring some of their forces from the Far Eastern front to the Pacific area in preparation for an attack on the British Empire outposts of Singapore, Hong Kong and Malaya and the American bases in the Pacific.

It was in following up this intelligence and seeking to establish the exact date and place from which the Japanese would launch their assault on the American bases that Sorge became atypically over-confident and paved the way to his downfall.

The Japanese by this time were convinced that there was a Russian spy who was sending radioed information to Moscow from somewhere in the Tokyo area. Their secret police decided to send out a girl agent named Kiyomi to get to know Sorge and keep a close watch on him.

Sorge should have been on his guard. Instead he became infatuated with the girl and took her around to restaurants with him. She was quick to notice that a waiter had passed him a message wrapped up in a ball of rice paper. The message contained a warning that the secret police were now hard on Sorge's trail.

Maybe by this time Sorge had decided that his network must be temporarily disbanded and that he must lie low for a while. All he was waiting for was the date of the Japanese proposed attack on Pearl Harbour. This he obtained, but instead of passing it on and then going underground immediately, he made another date with Kiyomi.

This was his second and finally fatal mistake. The girl alerted the secret police and the following day Sorge, together with his agents, was rounded up and arrested. The Russian spy network in Japan was destroyed.

The Germans, however, could not believe that Sorge was a guilty man and they appealed to the Japanese for his release on the grounds that their secret police had blundered.

To no avail: their pleas were rejected and Sorge was hanged on 7 November, 1944.

Nevertheless his achievements had been of enormous value to the Russians and it was estimated afterwards that the intelligence he provided for them was worth 'four divisions'.

August 1916. 8 inch Howitzers in action

Chapter 6

Spies of fiction

How many people have made up their minds to become – or at least to try to become – spies as a result of reading about the activities of fictional spies is anyone's guess. I should imagine the number is considerable, though possibly the vast majority rarely get beyond the stage of wishing.

In recent years the Russians have deliberately set out to glamourise their own spies, even those of modern times, by publishing a steady stream of books about them. They have also gone further than this by sponsoring a series of fictional spy stories which are part propaganda and probably partly an effort to make spying seem a respectable and patriotic career and to encourage recruitment.

It must be remembered that 'spy' has always been a somewhat dirty word in Russia, even when the spy is one of their own. For centuries the Russian people have become accustomed to the sneak informer who reports on their every activity. Now the authorities are trying to change this picture.

Apart from this the history of spy fiction has often been closely linked with the real life espionage game and novels about spies have had a positive effect on espionage. You can be fairly certain that today if any former Intelligence man writes a novel about spies, it will be carefully studied by other spy services in case it provides clues for them to follow up, or reveals techniques they do not know about. Similarly such books are also read by the spy-masters of the novelist's own Secret Service just in case he has been guilty of borrowing secret material from his own experiences.

One of the first writers to have inspired an Intelligence man was Edgar Allan Poe. True, he was not a writer of spy stories, but some of his works dealt with a subject closely allied to espionage – cryptography.

There is his famous short story, *The Gold Bug*, the action of which takes part in Sullivan's Island, near Charleston in

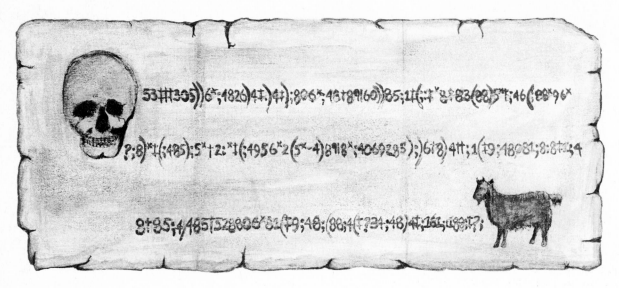

The Code in 'The Gold Bug'

South Carolina. A parchment was discovered and, when warm water was poured on it, lines of figures suddenly became visible. Poe then describes how two men worked together in trying to decipher the code, first finding out which characters and figures appeared most frequently and then applying them to those letters of the English language which seemed appropriate according to their frequency.

Poe gave a most detailed analysis of methods of deciphering and finally translated the message into: 'A good glass in the bishop's hostel in the devil's seat – forty-one degrees and thirteen minutes – northeast by north – main branch seventh limb east side – shoot from the left eye of the death's head – a beeline from the tree through the shot fifty feet out.'

This message still seemed almost totally obscure until the phrase 'bishop's hostel' was identified as referring to an ancient manor house on the island which had been inhabited by a family named Bessop. Eventually one of the oldest inhabitants of Sullivan's Island pointed out a rock that had once been known locally as Bessop's Castle.

This short story so inspired a young lieutenant named Cator in the British Admiralty that he decided to delve into all Poe's writings on cryptography. He came across an article in a Philadelphia weekly magazine in 1840 in which Poe claimed that there was no such thing as an unsolvable cipher and offered to solve any cipher messages sent to him. All he stipulated was that the messages should be in English and based on simple substitutions.

Poe received no fewer than a hundred such messages of varying length and one of these was from Lieutenant Cator who, however, did not send it under his own name but through an intermediary. Back came an accurate translation from Poe with the comment that it was an extremely difficult cryptogram, requiring a great deal of time to solve and possessing certain original features.

'I am impressed,' said Poe to Cator's intermediary, 'that anybody possessing the key to this cipher would have almost as much difficulty in making out the meaning as I did.'

Cator was as much impressed by Poe's criticisms as by his tributes. He had had no training in cipher work and there was then no Intelligence section at the Admiralty. Poe had succeeded in proving to him that the use of unusual words in compiling a cryptogram was quite common practice among amateur cryptographers. He also advised him to study French ciphers, claiming that the French were more advanced than the British in this respect. So Cator carried on his researches for another ten years and finally adapted the Vigenère cipher by completely reversing the Frenchman's encipherment process.

Alas, his diligent work does not seem to have brought him any reward. His notes and papers on the subject lay for years in an Admiralty file until in 1887 the admiral who was then organising the Naval Intelligence Department came across them and immediately acted on Cator's proposals.

Spy stories began to appear at the end of the nineteenth century and the early ones were neither good literature, nor particularly good entertainment. Most of them were melodramatic and crudely sensational of the 'goodie' versus the 'baddie' type, with the 'baddies' usually being of an inscrutable oriental type like the sinister Dr Fu Manchu. All of them lacked the realism and know-how of espionage shown by later writers.

Sir Arthur Conan Doyle was, of course, the doyen of the detective novel rather than of spy fiction, but in *The Bruce Partington Plans* and other stories he touched on espionage and brought in Sherlock Holmes to resolve what a baffled Secret Service could not cope with.

Nevertheless Conan Doyle's stories were eagerly read and even copied by two British spies. In *The Hound of the Baskervilles* Conan Doyle's villain, Stapleton, poses as a butterfly-collector. Sir Robert Baden-Powell, founder of the Boy Scout movement, adopted the same tactics when he went spying out the gun batteries in a Dalmatian fortress. He even made sketches of butterflies and worked in outlines of the fortifications in the drawings of their wings.

A E W Mason, author of a number of exciting romances himself, admitted that when he posed as a lepidopterist when engaged in espionage in Mexico he also got the idea from reading *The Hound of the Baskervilles*.

Some of the early spy story-writers such as William Le Queux actually wrote their books as a warning to the nation. Le Queux was obsessed with the menace of German spy networks operating inside Britain in the years before World War I. And Le Queux himself seems to have dabbled in the work of a secret agent, though in his case his imagination

Robert Stevens as Sherlock Holmes

A map of fortifications hidden in a sketch of a butterfly's wings

sometimes got the better of him and he tended in his reports to turn the most trivial incident into an insidious plot.

Indeed, it is surprising how many authors have been secret agents down the ages. In Shakespearean times there was Marlowe, who was probably murdered because of his espionage activities. Daniel Defoe has already been mentioned. There was also Matthew Prior, a poet, who organised a spy service in Paris in the days of the Stuart kings, and in World War I such illustrious authors as A E W Mason, Somerset Maugham, G K Chesterton, John Galsworthy, Thomas Hardy, Arnold Bennett and Conan Doyle all played their part in the Intelligence field.

In *Ashenden* Somerset Maugham created one of the earliest of modern spy fiction books. This was really a collection of stories about espionage experiences, thinly disguised as fiction, but actually based on Maugham's own work as a secret agent in World War I.

Ashenden, in fact, could be said to be the first realistic secret agent in fiction. He was not exactly an anti-hero, such as we have today, but he was not given to performing brilliant and courageous deeds. Ashenden was a worrier: he worried about missing trains and had an attack of nerves when a fellow agent was about to murder a Greek spy.

W Somerset Maugham. World famous British author and secret agent in World War I

Discussing the disparity between the romantic conception
of espionage and the dull, routine jobs he undertook,
Ashenden ruefully commented that 'the great chiefs of the
secret service in their London offices, their hands on the
throttle of this great machine, led a life full of excitement;
they moved their pieces here and there, they saw the pattern
woven by the multitudinous threads . . . but it must be
confessed that for the small fry like himself to be a member of
the secret service was not as adventurous an affair as the
public thought.

'Ashenden's official existence was as orderly and monotonous
as a City clerk's. He saw his spies at stated intervals and paid
them their wages; when he could get hold of a new one he
engaged him, gave him his instructions and sent him off
to Germany; he waited for the information that came through
and dispatched it; he went into France once a week to confer
with his colleague over the frontier and to receive his orders
from London; he visited the market-place on market-day to
get any messages the old butter-woman had brought him from
the other side of the lake; he kept his eyes and ears open;
and he wrote long reports which he was convinced no one read
till having inadvertently slipped a jest into one of them he
received a sharp rebuke for his levity. The work he was doing

**'M': James Bond's boss from
the film Dr. No**

was evidently necessary, but it could not be called anything but monotonous'.

Maugham joined the Red Cross in France during World War I as an ambulance driver and interpreter. Later he was recruited into the Secret Service and sent to Russia. He always felt that his mission in Russia was a total failure and he was often heard to assert in later life that if he could only have arrived six months sooner the Russian Revolution might have been prevented.

This may sound somewhat big-headed and in the light of history a totally arrogant statement. Yet history does not always record the ifs and buts of espionage and as far as the success or otherwise of revolutions it is often some unconsidered incident, some chance move that makes or mars it.

Maugham gave one clue in his book as to the real identity of Ashenden. The latter's superior officer once asks him: 'Where have you been living all these years?'
'At 36 Chesterfield Street, Mayfair,' is the reply. This was Maugham's own address before the war.

There is abundant evidence of Maugham's role as a secret agent in the private papers of Sir William Wiseman in Yale University Library. Sir William was controller of British Secret Service agents in the USA during World War I. From these papers it is evident that Maugham was an important agent in Russia in 1917.

One other interesting revelation in these papers is that Maugham's cover name was 'Somerville'. He also used this name as Ashenden's code-name in his novel.

Despite Maugham's attempt to portray Secret Service work as it really is, the fiction of the super-spy hero was maintained by such characters as 'Bulldog' Drummond in the immediate post-World War I years.

One way of getting information. Spy Chief talks to a butter seller in a French market

Chesterfield Street. Maugham lived there too

Maybe for would-be aspirants to the spy game the 'Bulldog' Drummonds and their ilk were models of what a good spy should be. In fact these characters were impossible prigs, snobs, prejudiced against all foreigners and of such little intellectual ability – or even sophistication – that in real life they would, as it were, be 'eaten before breakfast' and eliminated within twenty-four hours of attempting an assignment.

Today 'Bulldog' Drummond appears as a figure of fun, yet to an older generation he was the idol of his day. Not until Eric Ambler produced his *Mask of Demetrios* did we once again get a fictional spy who stood the test of authenticity and survived the test of realism.

By the time Ambler began to win readers by the million World War II was on us and spy thriller writers began to set their stories against the background of espionage in Europe. Bernard Newman caught the new mood of authenticity with such spy novels as *Maginot Line Murder*, *Death Under Gibraltar*, *Death to the Spy* and more especially in his collection of short stories – *Spy Catchers*.

This last book is still one of the best written around the subject of counter-espionage. Newman was especially good when dealing with the use of radio for code messages. In his story, *Spy by Music*, he tells of musical codes. There was a suspicion that the Germans were making use of these in their broadcasts. A team of experts started to study them and discovered that a musical alphabet was being used, allotting one or more letters to the minim.

'Yes, but he can't write a tune on long notes alone!' commented one of the experts.

'He might – a hymn. But he's connecting up dance tunes, so he has to do a fair amount of padding, linking up the "message" notes. Otherwise he would get no suitable melody at all – certainly not the improvisation this appears to be. An apparently pointless succession of minims might arouse suspicion – hence the padding, I should say –'

'Just a minute, old man. I like your professional enthusiasm and I'm very interested. But at the moment I'm more interested in results. What did this fellow say in his piano message?'

The musical improvisation was taken down, the musical alphabet applied to it and the letters written down below the musical notes. It read like this:

The musical code

It was then obvious that the message was: 'Convoy leaves Clyde Thursday'.

Another spy story writer at this time was Dennis Wheatley who not only possessed a strong realistic streak, but was actually so imaginative that, apart from writing such books, he found time to think out all kinds of espionage gimmicks to be tried out in the war.

His friends used jokingly to refer to it as 'Wheatley's War' and he was given an office in the underground fortress just off Whitehall as the only civilian member of the Joint Planning Staff.

After World War II there were so many real life espionage stories which could at last be told that for a long time the fiction writers did not stand any chance of competing successfully with reality. The first to do so was Ian Fleming with his creation of James Bond in the 1950's.

Bond was not an insular prig like 'Bulldog' Drummond, yet already by the standards of today he seems somewhat shadowy and unreal. Fleming had timed his creation of Bond to perfection. The public had been starved of a credible fictional spy hero for so long that they craved for someone who had an authentic background. Fleming, who had been assistant to the Director of Naval Intelligence at the British Admiralty in World War II, knew quite a lot about the spy game.

Unlike Maugham in an earlier war, Fleming had not been an agent in the field, but he did know how spies operated, how they were briefed and the background to the organisation behind a spy service. He also took great pains to supplement his knowledge by a great deal of travel and research.

James Bond was essentially a 'Cold War' warrior: all the Fleming stories were set against the espionage conflicts of the 'fifties and 'sixties and because they were so absolutely up-to-date in this respect their appeal was heightened.

Ian Fleming, author of the 007 books, with a gun

Sean Connery as James Bond

Fleming had a great love of mischief and often put real people into his James Bond stories just for a laugh. But also, with tongue in cheek, he sometimes wrote into his books a good deal of real life espionage, usually designed to keep the Russians guessing. For Bond's life was mainly spent in fighting the forces of the KGB and *Smersh*, Russia's dreaded 'Murder Brigade', or 'Terror and Diversion Branch'.

The James Bond books were compulsory reading inside the KGB and, to counteract what they called the 'cult of the decadent Western spy', the Russians persuaded a Bulgarian writer to produce a 'counter-Bond' hero of the Soviet Union whose task was to defeat the redoubtable James.

Then, in the 'sixties, came the advent of the 'anti-hero' in spy fiction. It was in part a reaction against James Bond and the superhuman antics of the 'men from UNCLE'. Realism had gone a long way, but not far enough, and the aim then became to make spies more like ordinary people with human weaknesses and possessing that commonest of all defects – fear.

So we had a succession of unheroic spies – the frightened spy, the inefficient spy, the mean spy and the double-crossing spy. The most successful book of this era was John Le Carré's *The Spy Who Came in From the Cold*. It was the story of a frustrated British agent who decided, after his sub-agents in East Germany had been liquidated, to go behind the Iron Curtain to destroy the master mind who had directed these killings and ruined a segment of the British intelligence network. In the end he is brutally discarded by his own Secret Service and slithers deeper into drinking and destitution and eventually to death.

So realistic was Le Carré's first book that this, plus the fact that the name he used on the title cover was a pseudonym – his real name is David Cornwell – caused the Russians to

Roger Moore as James Bond

Richard Burton as 'The Spy who came in from the Cold'

One of the dreaded SMERSH agents

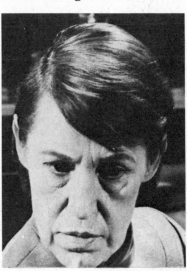

allege in their *Literary Gazette* that the author had been a British intelligence agent himself.

It was then that Le Carré revealed his true identity, blandly replying to the legend that he stole his plot from secret files back in 1948 that in that year 'I was an enterprising spy – aged sixteen. But there were extenuating circumstances. I'm also the son of Groucho Marx and Mata Hari!'

Richard Burton at the Berlin Wall

Chapter 7

British spies turn fiction into fact

From fictional spies it seems perfectly natural to turn to the British Secret Service and not merely because the British seem to have had a monopoly of best-selling spy thriller writers. The truth is that the conventional, prosaic British have been most unconventional and least prosaic when it comes to espionage.

It would not be stretching too fine a point to say that they have consistently turned fiction into fact. Their very special and almost unique quality has been a gift for dreaming up situations and then proceeding to create them in real life.

The ploy is really quite simple. All it requires to make it succeed is a vivid imagination and great attention to the minutest details. It works like this: the top men in the Secret Service ask themselves what would most embarrass or deceive a potential enemy to a disastrous effect. Having found the answer to this they pass the problem down to their ideas men. The latter work out a project in the form of a rough imaginative outline. This outline is given to a planning team who begin to work out all the details by which the plan can be put into effect.

As has already been seen many British writers of spy fiction have themselves been engaged in the Intelligence game. Writers generally have never been honoured in Britain as they are, for example, in France where streets are named after them. But spy thriller writers have invariably been welcomed with eagerness by the British Secret Service.

Of all Secret Services in the world there is probably none which has been so inconsistent as the British. On top of the world in the Elizabethan era, it toppled under the early Stuarts, but rose again to great efficiency under Cromwell so that Sagredo, the Venetian Ambassador in London at that time, declared that 'there is no government on earth which divulges its affairs less than England, or is more punctually informed of those of the others.'

Sir Richard Burton. One of the great explorers of the 19th century

The British Secret Service tends to slip back into slackness and incompetence in peace time, but inevitably responds to the challenge of war, or impending war, with a brilliance and originality which still make it one of the most respected in the world even now that it is no longer the service of a super-power.

More than in any other Secret Service it has relied on the individual agent of outstanding merit. It is said that the British love amateurs. Certainly their best spies have usually been gifted, eccentric amateurs rather than trained professionals. Such a spy was Sir Richard Burton, the explorer and translator of *The Arabian Nights* and other oriental works.

Whenever Burton went off on his exploratory trips in Africa, Asia or the Middle East he collected an enormous amount of intelligence. In fact Burton's real value to the Secret Service of that period was that he went to places no European had visited before. As a young subaltern in India he first engaged in work as a spy by disguising himself as a native Moslem, opening three small shops in Karachi and, by speaking the local dialect, obtaining information from his customers.

Burton's note-books reveal what a keen observer he was of the smallest detail. He wrote out in text-book fashion the methods of fighting used by the Moslems, made drawings and notes of their various weapons, their customs, habits and even their talismans.

Prior to each of the last two world wars Britain has tended to let its Secret Service run down and to reduce the amount of money allotted to it. Therefore when war has come there has been a desperate need for recruitment of men of ability. It is then that the talented amateur has come into his own, sometimes late in life.

A E W Mason, previously the author of romantic novels (later to turn his experiences to good account in spy thrillers), was fifty when he was recruited into the Naval Intelligence Department in World War I. He would, on account of his age, have been given a desk job, but, perhaps because he had imbued some of the romantic qualities of his own fictional heroes, he demanded action in the field.

Reference has already been made to some of his work as a spy, but it should perhaps be mentioned that this veteran who had never had any training in the spy game operated over a number of years in Mexico, Morocco and Spain. In Mexico he discovered that the Germans were using a wireless station at Ixtapalapa, so he recruited a team of three Mexicans and put the station out of action by destroying the audion lamps on which they were dependent and which were in short supply.

His greatest coup was in Spain where he learned of a plot by the Germans to spread the disease anthrax on the Western

Shaving brushes that could have been deadly

Front among the Allies by infecting shaving brushes and then importing them from Spain to France. Mason managed to intercept a consignment of these shaving brushes and so alerted the Allies to the danger.

But it was in World War II in which the Secret Service, aided and abetted by other branches of Intelligence, developed to perfection the theme-title of this chapter – turning fiction into fact.

It was really a case of depending almost entirely on brains and imagination in a situation in which Britain could do very little else in a war against a nation that had captured France, Holland, Belgium, Denmark, Norway, Poland, Czechoslovakia and Rumania, and had Italy as an ally.

In the early summer of 1940 Britain had only the narrow English Channel to save her from instant defeat by the Germans. Her only Allies then were distant countries like Canada, Australia, South Africa and New Zealand. Her spy networks inside Europe had been largely, though not totally, put out of action by the German advance.

Two immediate tasks presented themselves. One was to try to bluff the Germans that Britain was stronger than she really was and by this means to dissuade her from attempting a cross-Channel invasion by sea. The other was to feed the enemy with false information which would keep him guessing.

In both of these tasks the British genius for improvisation and imaginative planning achieved astonishing results. Here again there was a link between mystery, thriller and spy fiction writers and the Secret Service. One of them was J C Masterman (now Sir John Masterman), one time Vice-Chancellor of Oxford University.

Masterman started writing mystery stories in the early 'thirties. In his book *Fate Cannot Harm Me* (1935) he almost forecast his future work in the foreword to it when he wrote that 'breaking rules is fun, and the middle-aged and respectable have in this regard a capacity for innocent enjoyment at least as great as that of the youthful and rebellious'.

Years later Masterman wrote another book, *The Case of the Four Friends* in which he described the case of a double agent named Bannister: 'Portugal was neutral and so to Portugal came the agents official and unofficial of many countries and countries on both sides. It was not possible to learn in Berlin what was happening in London, but it might well be possible to hear, or to guess, or deduce in neutral Portugal what was happening in both. And further, it might be possible to spread information (and make it appear credible) of what was *not* happening in London or Berlin and yet have it believed in the other place. And so Lisbon became a kind of international clearing-ground, a busy ant-heap of spies and agents, where political and military secrets and information – true and false, but mainly false – were bought and sold and where men's brains were pitted against each other. There was, of course, more in it than this. The life of the secret agent is dangerous enough, but the life of the double-agent is infinitely more precarious. If anyone balances on a swinging tight-rope it is he, and a single slip must send him crashing to destruction. Bannister went to Lisbon ostensibly in a commercial capacity, and he was well-known and respected in British and allied diplomatic and business circles – but he was much more than that.'

Masterman's job, when war came, meant thinking up the same kind of characters he had written about in his novels and then choosing people to fit the roles provided. Known as the 'Double-Cross System', it involved the creation of double-agents to feed false information to the enemy.

A special committee to plan the details of this system set up a variety of targets so that afterwards Masterman could claim with some justice that 'for the greater part of the war we did much more than practise a large-scale deception through

double-agents: by means of the double-agent we actively ran
and controlled the German espionage system in this country'.

The aims were to infiltrate the enemy's spy networks, to
capture any new spies who came to Britain, to get details of the
German code and cipher systems, to send back false information to the enemy by captured enemy agents' radio transmitters and to deceive the Germans about British war plans.

The code names given to these double-agents sound like
something out of a comic picture strip – Mutt and Jeff, Snow,
Zig-Zag, Garbo, Balloon, Bronx, Carrot, Careless, Celery,
Dragonfly, Lipstick, Peppermint, Sweet William, the Worm
and Washout. All these were acting a part and were briefed
in the minutest detail as to how they should behave, what
characteristics they should develop: it was almost like a play
producer coaching his actors in their parts.

There were about forty of these 'double-cross' agents, some
of whom were inevitably failures. For example, 'Weasel' was
dropped because he was suspected of having warned the
Germans what was going on. Another refused to continue to
work for the British, while one was dismissed for 'suspicious
and bad communications'.

Yet there were several successes, more than enough to
deceive the Germans and to destroy most of their attempts to
infiltrate agents to Britain. 'Garbo' proved to be a gifted
writer of prolific reports which altogether filled fifty volumes
in the secret files in London. He was a Spaniard, equally
hostile to communism and fascism, who was one of the most
effective of all agents. Curiously, when he volunteered to serve
the British in January, 1941, he was rejected. Undeterred by
this rebuff, he boldly offered his services to the Germans, pretending that he was in a position to go to Britain to spy for them.

Having been accepted by the Germans, he disappeared
from Madrid with a questionnaire, secret ink and cover
addresses. For nine months he stayed in Lisbon and sent to
the Germans letters supposedly written in England and
conveyed by courier to Portugal for posting. His reports to the
enemy were almost entirely fictitious, but nonetheless
convincing.

Eventually he informed the British how he had been fooling
the Germans and taking their money and 'Garbo' was then
taken over and controlled by British Intelligence. His personal
credit remained high with both his real and his pseudo-friends
and the British awarded him an MBE and the Germans an
Iron Cross.

'Garbo' sent in equally lengthy reports to the Germans:
in all they received from him some 400 secret letters and
2,000 long radio messages. In 1943 it became important to
mislead the Germans as to the actual point at which the
Allied landings in Normandy the following year were to be
made. To try to convince the enemy that the assault would be

made from South-East England across the narrow Straits of Dover, 'Garbo' sent them details of fictitious extensions to the Chislehurst Caves in Kent, suggesting that an arms depot and a communications centre were to be set up here.

One of the first of these 'double-cross' agents was 'Snow', an electrical engineer who had frequently been to Germany on business and brought back with him a certain amount of technical information which was passed to British Intelligence. This information resulted in 'Snow' being recruited as a permanent agent.

'Snow' somewhat complicated matters by playing his own highly dangerous game as a double-agent long before the 'double-cross' system had been introduced. He established contact with the Germans, offering his services to them while at the same time admitting that he had been working for the British.

When the British authorities learned of this 'Snow' was rigorously cross-examined. His story was that he had deliberately set out to infiltrate the German Secret Service on behalf of the British. No action was taken against him. The authorities decided to take a gamble with 'Snow' and he was allowed to carry on as a German agent until war broke out.

In August, 1939, a month before the war began, 'Snow' returned to Germany in company with two suspected recruits for German Intelligence. He came back to London the following month, telephoned an inspector of the Special (Police) Branch and made a date to meet him at Waterloo Station. At that rendezvous 'Snow' was arrested and put in prison. Once there he told the authorities where he had hidden a secret German transmitter and suggested it should be brought to him in prison so that he could get in touch with the Germans under British control.

His request was granted and 'Snow' not only got into contact with the enemy from his cell, but provided some useful information, including details of a Welsh Nationalist organisation which the Germans proposed to utilise for carrying out sabotage in Wales.

Through 'Snow' the British were able to discover three German agents actually operating in Britain. In addition he provided details of the German radio codes and cipher procedure. He was eventually released and sent on various assignments to the Continent. On one of these the Germans suggested to 'Snow' that he should find for them a new agent who could be brought to Germany to undergo training in sabotage and spying. He was asked by the Germans to obtain a trawler and to rendezvous with either a German submarine or aircraft in the North Sea.

'Snow' informed the British who provided a trawler and also the new 'agent', code-name 'Biscuit', a man who had been a petty thief and drug smuggler, but who had nevertheless become a reliable informant and appeared to have reformed. Not surprisingly, however, 'Biscuit' was extremely suspicious of 'Snow' and thought he might be led into a trap.

These suspicions were heightened when two days before the date fixed for the rendezvous a plane appeared and gave the agreed recognition signal. 'Biscuit' decided to take charge of the situation: he ordered the trawler's lights to be extinguished and for it to return home, at the same time insisting that 'Snow' was imprisoned in his cabin.

There were some doubts after this as to exactly what game 'Snow' was playing, a quandary which can befall the most faithful of double-agents in certain circumstances. Only time could prove whose side he was on and eventually the British authorities were certain that 'Snow' was serving his masters in London satisfactorily.

Other 'double-cross' agents were 'Sweet William', a British subject employed at the Spanish Embassy who was used to send espionage messages through the diplomatic bag; 'The Snark', a Yugoslav domestic servant who reported on underground food stores; and 'Basket', an Irishman who was landed near Dublin by parachute to act as a double-agent.

It was indisputably due to such agents as these that the German High Command were led to believe that the Allies were to land in Greece and not North Africa and in the Bay of Biscay and the Calais area instead of in Normandy.

But of all the pieces of spy fiction which were translated into reality by the Secret Service in World War II none was so bizarre as the case of 'The Man Who Never Was'.

This operation – for it was so complex and detailed that it required the title of an operation – was somewhat ghoulishly called 'Mincemeat'. Its aim was to convince the German High Command that the Allies were planning a major assault on Greece in the autumn of 1942 and not on North Africa.

It was absolutely vital that this story should be believed by the Germans and acted upon. Thus a mere infiltration of rumours or gossip through the usual 'double-cross' agents was not enough. Information leaked in this manner would be carefully checked and, if there was no supporting evidence, probably discarded.

How, then, was the best way to convince the enemy? Various plans were submitted by the ideas men in Intelligence, but all were discounted as not being sufficiently credible. Then by a lucky chance one of the planners started reading through some Intelligence reports. One of them, sent from an agent in Cadiz, told how a British plane had crashed into the sea and a body from it had been washed up on the coast of Spain. There were some papers on the body – fortunately not of great value to the enemy – and these had been shown to the Germans by the Spanish police.

'This must be our best method of planting the information,'

**'The Man who never Was'
being prepared**

argued the ideas man. 'We now know, what we have suspected for some time, that the Spaniards keep the Germans informed on such matters and pass on information to them.

'We must see that another body gets washed up on a Spanish beach and that this time it contains the information we want the Germans to have.'

The idea was not accepted with any unanimity at the start. It was argued that the first problem was to obtain a body – no easy task in a democracy – and that the second was to ensure that it did not sink, but was washed up on Spanish territory. So the whole project was handed over to a small group of planners, in which the Twenty Committee (those in charge of the 'double-cross' system), the Secret Service, Army, Navy and Air Force Intelligence Services were involved.

Details of the plan were eventually put forward primarily by two officers, (Lieut-Cdr) Ewen Montagu, Naval Intelligence,

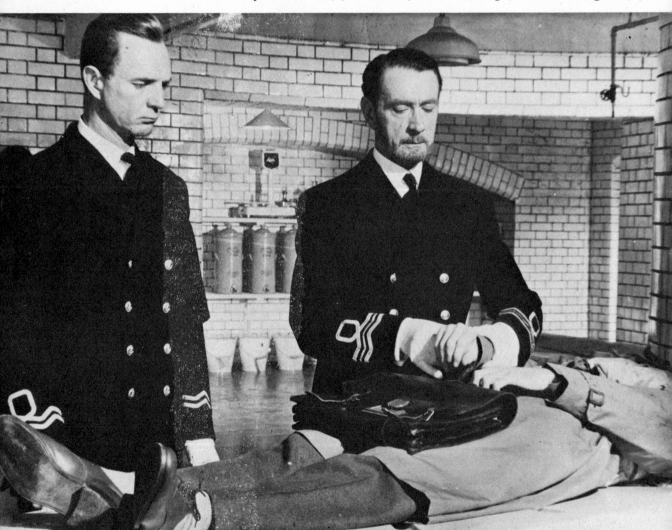

The body is ready for the container

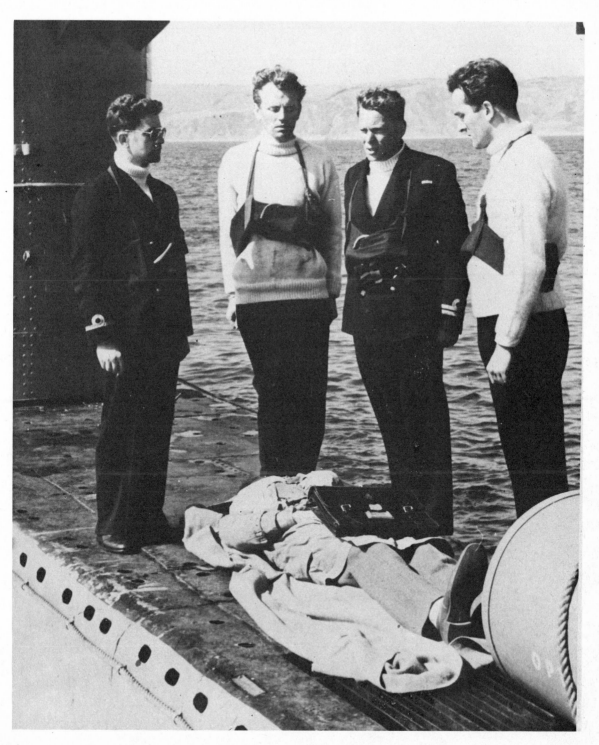

The capsule containing 'optical instruments' on its way to the submarine

and (Flight-Lieut) Cholmondeley. It was decided to create a fictitious character whose identity was to be given to the body which was to be dispatched to a Spanish beach. The name given was that of 'Major Martin, Royal Marines' and great care was taken to ensure that if the Germans started checking up on his credentials there would be sufficient evidence to satisfy them.

'Major Martin' was even provided with a real life girl friend – she is still alive – and a photograph of her and letters of hers were to be planted on his body. There was also a bank statement to show he had an overdraft of £79 19s 2d. Had the Germans wished to make inquiries of this 'girl friend' they could easily have done so, without discovering that she was a party to the plot. An obituary notice for Major Martin was prepared for publication in the Press.

Ewen Montagu has told this story in great detail in his

book, *The Man Who Never Was.* What he did not reveal was how the planners got hold of a body. Of course, in some totalitarian countries they would not have been so squeamish about finding a body quickly. Probably they would actually have murdered a soldier if he would have made a convincing 'corpse' whose identity would have impressed an enemy. But Montagu turned to his friend, Sir William Bentley-Purchase, the Coroner for St Pancras in London, whose job it was to inquire into deaths and who had ready access to the mortuary.

'You can't get bodies just for the asking,' said Sir William. 'Even with bodies all over the place, each has to be accounted for.'

Just any corpse would not have done. It had to be that of a man of the same age, height and weight as the mythical 'Major Martin' and one which, even after death, would have passed for an ex-Major of the Royal Marines.

A body to fit these requirements was selected. Most bodies in mortuaries are those of persons killed in road accidents, or who have died as the result of a fall, suicide, or even murder. They needed the body of a man who would appear to have drowned, for they were well aware that the enemy would want a post-mortem on the corpse.

Even when they had obtained the body there were problems. Permission of the dead man's relatives had to be obtained and then they had to be sworn to secrecy. Sir Bernard Spilsbury, an eminent pathologist, had to be consulted on the best means of ensuring that the man would seem to have been drowned. Then the corpse had to be taken from the deep-freeze and fitted with the major's uniform and there were difficulties about getting his boots over his frozen limbs. The feet had to be thawed by an electric fire and then, when 'Major Martin' was fully attired, he had to be put back into refrigeration again.

Various documents and letters, all faked by the planning staff, were planted on the body, including a letter from the Vice-Chief of the General Staff to General Alexander explaining that a landing in Greece was being planned. All the documents were put in a black official Government briefcase which was to be hitched to the body with a light chain. As a last thought two stubs of theatre tickets for 22 April were put in his pocket so that it should be clear that he had only very recently flown out from London, as he could not have been at a London theatre on that date if he had travelled by sea. It was important for the Germans to believe that the intelligence they would receive was of immediate date.

In a large container marked 'Handle with Care: Optical Instruments' the body was placed aboard the submarine *Seraph* and the crew, having been sworn to secrecy, dropped the body in the sea about a mile from the beach at Huelva. The planning team had chosen Huelva because it was known that the Germans had a highly competent spy organisation in that area and the final problem had been to make sure that the body was deposited in such a position that the tide would carry it to the shore. Tide tables and information on currents had been supplied by the Admiralty.

The Spaniards found the body and the Germans were supplied with copies of the documents. They believed them to be genuine and the result was that when the Allied build-up of shipping appeared at Gibraltar prior to the landings in North Africa the Germans were still expecting an attack on Greece.

Yet the planners' work was not finished even then. The deception was maintained: 'Major Martin's' name appeared in the list of casualties published and when the Spaniards informed the British of the finding of the body a funeral was staged on Spanish soil and a tombstone erected to his memory at Huelva.

Indeed, but for the curiosity of a journalist regarding this tombstone, the story of 'Major Martin' might never have been known. He thought it was curious that in war time a tombstone should have been put up to the memory of an officer on foreign soil so quickly. He started to make inquiries locally and gradually built up at least part of this bizarre tale. It was not all that difficult for him as years before he had done some spying himself.

Major William Martin's actual grave in Spain. The man in the picture helped his father to dig the grave. The inscription reads: 'William Martin. Born 29th March 1907, died 24th April 1943. Beloved son of John Glyndwyr Martin and the late Antonia Martin of Cardiff, Wales'

Chapter 8

The patient probe of the KGB

Russia throughout the ages has been obsessed with spying. This may be due in part to a quirk in national characteristics, but historically it can be traced back centuries to when Genghis Khan, bent on conquering Europe as well as Asia, descended on Russia, always sending his spies ahead of his armies.

The Mongols dominated Russia for two and a half centuries and they enforced their rule by a ruthless system of police spies and informers. They were finally expelled and succeeded by yet another bloodthirsty tyrant, Ivan the Terrible, who, though rescuing the Russians from one peril, put them in thrall once more to his own dreaded secret police, the Oprichniki.

All the Czars since that date developed espionage in one form or another. Mainly it was to protect themselves and consisted of internal spying on the Russian people. Sometimes they introduced harsh secret police systems, at others they tried to win popularity by abolishing the secret police, merely bringing in rather less obvious methods of spying.

The yellow box outside the Winter Palace

One Czar, Paul, hit on the idea of giving all his people a chance to spy. Outside his Winter Palace he placed a Yellow Box into which any of his subjects were invited to put letters containing intelligence, or even to make allegations of treachery or to denounce enemies of the state.

Paul, however, was not discriminating in his assessment of such haphazard and amateurish intelligence. He was apt to overlook important information, but to order the arrest of an officer who had been reported for being improperly dressed.

The most powerful espionage system employed by the Czars was that of the Ochrana introduced by Nicholas I. This was primarily aimed at keeping a watch on the growing number of revolutionary organisations which began to spring up in Russia about the middle of the nineteenth century.

**One of the disguises
assumed by Russian agents**

Once again its aim was, like that of its predecessors, to turn Russia into a nation of spies, to encourage, threaten and bribe people to spy on their neighbours, sons to spy on their fathers, and to try to ensure that there was a spy in every family.

Horrible and ruthless though this was, it was not particularly efficient. For such a system to work it requires the professional officers of the Secret Service to be watched and subjected to the same terror that they use on other people. The Ochrana officials were more or less immune from such dangers.

Such a system was terribly extravagant. It meant that Russia was spending more on espionage than any other nation in the world at a time when her people as a whole were impoverished and, compared with the rest of Europe, virtually slaves. Parkinson's Law began to operate: when you get a hundred thousand or more people sending in regular reports you need a larger staff to sift all the material.

And as the Ochrana became larger, so its standards dropped. A great deal of time was wasted in studying worthless reports. Many revolutionaries were captured and sent to prison, but there were always new recruits to take their place. The new members were forewarned and developed a cunning that enabled them to defeat the Ochrana. They began by feeding them with false information and finally they themselves began to infiltrate the Ochrana.

There was also one other serious fault in the organisation of the Ochrana which in the end proved fatal to it. When a new Minister of the Interior was appointed in the Russian Government he retired the head of the Ochrana and put his own favourite in his place. Such changes occurred so frequently that they interfered with the efficiency of the secret police, especially as the retiring head of the Ochrana often took his secrets and files with him and did not pass them on to his successor.

By the turn of the century Russia was faced with a serious problem in that there were several revolutionary organisations which not only operated inside their country, but had organised cells in foreign territory. Thus Russian spying outside the country was concentrated on tracking down revolutionaries in exile in Zurich, Geneva, Brussels, Paris, London and Rome.

An Ochrana professional agent, as distinct from an informer, was expected to be a versatile operator. He had to memorise the names of all the streets in the area in which he worked, as well as the timetables and the times at which factories opened and closed each day. One essential qualification was that he should be able to drive a horse and cab like a professional, as agents were often required to pose as cab-drivers as a means of watching suspects.

The Ochrana agent had to make a report not only of what he had seen each day but exactly how he had spent his time down to the minutest detail. This training resulted in time-consuming reports of which eighty per cent was often totally irrelevant to the real job of espionage.

Lyov Tolstoy showed up the ridiculous nature of many of these reports when he described how in 1897 he had been shadowed by the Ochrana all the time he was in St Petersburg. At this time Tolstoy was one of the most illustrious figures in Russia's literary world and not engaging in any activities which were a danger to the state. Yet on his file card the Ochrana had recorded what he wore, what tobacco he smoked, what he bought in the shops, what he had for his meals and how much they cost and even to which people he raised his hat!

The case of Ievno Azeff has been mentioned in an earlier chapter. There is little doubt that he was a double-agent in the worst sense of the word. He was anxious to make as much money as he could as a highly successful Ochrana agent, but at the same time he seems to have been equally anxious to play a role as a revolutionary, organising the assassinations of prominent people and then betraying his own fellow-plotters. He even went to Glasgow to persuade a member of the crew of a Russian cruiser to attempt to shoot the Czar. The attempt failed, but it ended Azeff's career both as a revolutionary and an Ochrana agent. Azeff himself escaped and after travelling round the world eventually settled in Berlin, always dreading discovery by the revolutionaries more even than by the Ochrana. But when the facts about Azeff's career were discovered the Ochrana was never the same again. Attempts were made to hush up the whole affair, but it all ended with nobody trusting anybody else.

The case of Azeff leads us on to the revolution of 1917 and the creation by the Communists of a new and more efficient secret police – the Cheka.

Though they started from scratch the Communists had one great advantage: as revolutionaries for many years constantly at war with the Ochrana they had had every opportunity of studying the methods of the latter and knowing its weaknesses. Some of them – even Stalin himself, it is said – had played a double-game of infiltrating the Ochrana and becoming police agents themselves. Unlike Azeff, however, they had consistently worked for their own cause alone.

The Communists therefore realised how a vast secret police network was vulnerable to counter-revolutionary movements and they decided that the only efficient manner in which this risk could be combatted was by blackmail, terror and the killing of all suspects. The Ochrana had to a limited

Stalin

extent employed such tactics, but nothing in modern history, except perhaps in Nazi Germany, has equalled the excesses of the Cheka.

The full title of the Cheka was Extraordinary Commission for the Struggle against Counter-Revolution and Sabotage. Its first head was Felix Dzershinsky, the son of a Polish aristocrat who had served many years in the revolutionary ranks. He spelt out his policy to the Council of People's Commissars very clearly: 'We stand for organised terror . . . Terror is an absolute necessity during times of revolution . . . even if sometimes it falls on the heads of the innocent.'

A British spy, Sir Paul Dukes, who was operating in Russia under various disguises at this time, gave a first-hand account of the work of the Cheka. 'Trials were summary,' he wrote. 'The Cheka had neither the time nor the inclination to unravel the rights and wrongs of charges against those whom they denounced as "bourgeois parasites" . . . The usual procedure was to line the victims up against the wall blindfolded and to shoot them, sometimes in batches by machine-gun fire.'

Felix Dzershinsky. Chief of Russian Intelligence. 1917

Out of this crude secret police there gradually emerged a system of espionage that was brilliantly conceived, subtle and, above all, patient. As far as effective espionage outside Russia was concerned it took the best part of ten years to build up. Yet by the late 'twenties it was already the most dreaded spy service to the Western world.

How was this achieved? It was the result of haphazard, hastily improvised espionage on the one hand and patient long-term planning on the other. The first method resulted in a few quick successes, large-scale recruiting and then a whole series of blunders which called for drastic re-organisation in the 'thirties. The second method took nearly thirty years to bear results.

In 1917-22 the quickest way to become a Soviet spy for a foreigner was to join the Communist Party. One must remember that in this euphoric period of the revolution some in Russia believed that fellow-Communists in Britain, France, Germany and Hungary might seize power and extend the revolution. Therefore an attempt was made to recruit Communists in foreign countries.

In this way Jean Cremet, a leading French Communist, became chief of the Soviet Intelligence network in France and through his initiative cells of spies were set up among workers in France's armament factories, while Ernst Wollweber, a German, was one of the chief agents in Hamburg where he recruited Communist seamen as spies.

But gradually the Western powers became aware of the menace inside their countries and in Britain, France and elsewhere arrests of suspects were carried out. The French rounded up a whole network, while the British raided the

Leon Trotsky. 1879–1940

ЛЕВ ДАВИДОВИЧ ТРОЦКИЙ,

offices of the Soviet Trade delegation in London and from documents found there discovered that this place was being used as a headquarters for Russian espionage in Britain.

It then dawned on the Russians that they needed to change their policy. First of all, any member of a foreign Communist Party who spied for them was liable to be known to the counter-intelligence service of his country and therefore liable to be watched. Secondly, the fact that a man was a Communist might ensure his loyalty to the Soviet cause, but it did not mean he would make a good spy. In fact many of the Communist agents were bungling amateurs.

So the emphasis for external spying was put on professionalism. Recruits must be trained before they were put in the field. Such agents were warned not to have any links with the Communist Party or its members in the country in which they operated. Before they were sent abroad they were given a tough and highly technical course at one of the new schools for spies.

By this time the Cheka had been superseded by the GPU and a new espionage network, the Fourth Bureau of the Red Army, more generally known as the GRU, was set up. The GPU underwent many purges and changes in its personnel after Dzershinsky died until it was eventually succeeded by the NKVD and finally by the KGB, which is the chief espionage organisation today. The GRU has always been a highly efficient military intelligence service and it managed to survive the expulsion of Trotsky, its founder, from the Soviet high command. Richard Sorge was an example of the best type of GRU agent.

I have already described Soviet espionage in this chapter's title as a 'patient probe'. No other spy service in the world has shown the same penchant for planning not just a few years ahead, but in some cases for twenty or thirty years.

We saw in chapter one how Konon Molody's career in espionage was planned from the early age of eleven, and how more than thirty years later he was operating as a top Soviet agent. A girl of fourteen, the daughter of a Soviet spy and a Frenchwoman, born in Moscow, was sent to Tangier in 1937 to be kept in reserve for spying operations during World War II. No doubt she was always kept under observation during her probationary period which was spent as a maid-servant in the Hotel Rif, which the Gestapo had taken over as their headquarters in Tangier. Her chance came in 1943 when she was sent to Algiers as a fully-fledged professional operator.

The Russian view of building up an agent is that from an early age he must be given a new identity and even a new personality. It is curious that for a nation which is characterised as being ultra-suspicious of foreigners they take great risks in employing foreigners and often give preference to a Russian citizen who has one foreign parent.

The Russian revolutionary Rudolf Ivanovich Abel. Imprisoned in America for 30 years, but exchanged for Gary Powers in 1962

Sorge, for example, had a German father and Colonel Rudolf Abel, one of their ace spies of the past twenty years, was reported after his death to have had some British ancestry. This has never been admitted by the Russians who say he was born in St Petersburg on 2 July, 1902, but his gravestone in Moscow suggests he was born in London. Certainly he lived in Britain and other European countries as a boy, for his father travelled around a great deal and took his son with him.

His father had been a minor official under the Czars, but young Abel had also helped his father to distribute Bolshevik propaganda. It was his fluent English and German which drew him to the attention of the authorities as well as the fact that radio-telegraphy was his hobby. He was recruited into the foreign espionage branch at an early age and early in World War II was operating in Switzerland.

Then, when the Americans uncovered a major group of atomic spies inside the United States in 1950 Abel was given a course in micro-photography and radio and wire-tapping and sent to Canada under the name of Andrew Kayotis. Soon after this he moved into the USA.

Abel was such a brilliant agent that ten years later Allen Dulles, then head of the CIA, said: 'I wish we had a couple like him in Moscow.' He was essentially a loner, self-sufficient, well versed in all the techniques of espionage and able to take charge of the whole American network.

In many respects the career of Abel is a model for any spy and when eventually he was caught it was entirely through the inefficiency of one of his sub-agents, a man whom he had mistrusted and asked Moscow to replace. They did not heed Abel's warning.

Wishing to be as unobtrusive as possible, Abel created for himself the personality of a recluse, a man who had only a few friends, did his own cooking and whose recreations were visiting museums and concerts. The cover name he took in New York was that of Emil Goldfus, an artist, moving mainly

The microdot found in Mrs Kroger's handbag Opposite: The same microdot enlarged

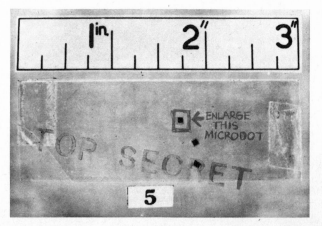

9/XII—60г. ЗДРАВСТВУЙ, ДОРОГОЙ И ХОРОШИЙ МОЙ! ПОЗДРАВЛЯЮ ...Я С ПРОШЕДШИМ
ПРАЗДНИКОМ 43-Й ГОДОВЩИНОЙ ОКТЯБРЯ. ЖДАЛА ОТ ТЕБЯ ПИСЬМА,НО ОКАЗАЛОСЬ, ЧТО
ВОЗМОЖНО БУДЕТ В ЭОМ МЕСЯЦЕ. НА РАБОТЕ У МЕНЯ ВСЕ ХОРОШО. СРЕДИ МОИХ
УЧЕНИЦ ЕСТЬ РУМЫНСКИЕ ДЕВОЧКИ 7 И 8 ЛЕТ. И ВОТ Я ВЗЯЛА НА СЕБЯ ЗАДАЧУ, ИЗУ-
ЧИТЬ ИХ РУССКОЙ АЗБУКЕ. УСПЕХИ КОЛОССАЛЬНЫЕ (КОНЕЧНО, ЗАСЛУГИ ДЕВОЧЕК) НА-
ВЗАИМНО ОНИ МЕНЯ "УЧАТ" РУМЫНСКОМУ. ПРИ ОБХОДЕ НЕКОТОРОЙ КОМИССИЕЙ ОНИ
ТАК ХОРОШО ЧИТАЛИ, ЧТО МНЕ КАК-ТО ХОРОШО И ПРИЯТНО СТАЛО НА ДУШЕ. ТЕПЕРЬ ПРИ
КАЖДОМ МОЕМ ПОЯВЛЕНИИ ОНИ МЕНЯ СПРАШИВАЮТ, А БУДУ ЛИ Я ИХ УЧИТЬ ЕЩЕ?!! В ВО-
СКРЕ БЫЛ У НАС ВЕЧЕР НА РАБОТЕ,НА КОТОРОМ Я ПЕЛА "ЖУРАВЛИ" И ПРОЧИЕ. ВСПОМ-
НИЛА НАШУ ЖИЗНЬ В ПРАГЕ И КАК-ТО СТАЛО ГРУСТНО-ГРУСТНО. ВЕДЬ СКОЛЬКО МЫ
ВСТРЕЧАЕМСЯ,ВСЕ НАМ ПРИХОДИТСЯ КУДА-ТО СПЕШИТЬ И ВСЕ У НАС НЕ ХВАТАЕТ ВРЕ-
МЕНИ: ВСПОМНИЛА ПРЕДПОСЛЕДНИЙ ДЕНЬ, ПРОВЕДЕННЫЙ В ПРАГЕ, А ОСОБЕННО УТРОМ
МНЕ НЕ ДАЮТ ПОКОЯ, КАК-ТО ТЯЖЕЛО И ГРУСТНО СТАЛО ИХ ПЕТЬ. ДОМА У НАС ВСЕ ПО-
СТАРОМУ. ЛИЗА МЕНЯ В ЭТОЙ ЧЕТВЕРТИ ОЧЕНЬ ОГОРЧИЛА.ПЕРВЫЙ РАЗ ЗА ВСЮ ЕЕ
УЧЕБУ ЛИЗА ПРИНЕСЛА 4-Е ТРОЙКИ: ПО ГЕОМЕТРИИ, АЛГЕБРЕ, АНГЛИЙСКОМУ И ФИЗКУЛЬ-
ТУРЕ, ОСТАЛЬНЫЕ ЧЕТВЕРКИ. ТЫ НЕ ПРЕДСТАВЛЯЕШЬ, КАК Я РАССТРОИЛАСЬ, ВЕДЬ ЕЙ ЗА
ГОДОМ ИНСТИТУТ. ДИМА ПРИНЕС ЕЩЕ ХУЖЕ ОТМЕТКИ, ВКЛЮЧАЯ ДИСЦИПЛИНУ И ПРИЛЕЖА-
НИЕ. 7-ОГО Я БЫЛА У РИМЫ И ИГОРЯ, ВЕЧЕР ПРОШЕЛ ОЧЕНЬ ХОРОШО. БЫЛО 14 ЧЕЛОВЕК.
ДАЖЕ ТРОЙНЯК. ВЫПИЛИ ЗА ТЕБЯ, ВСЕ ТЕБЯ ВСПОМИНАЮТ ДОБРЫМИ СЛОВАМИ. ПО
НАСТОЯНИЮ И ПРОСЬБЕ МАРИНЫ И ВСЕХ ПРИСУТСТВУЮЩИХ Я СПЕЛА-ОПЯТЬ-ТАКИ "ЖУРАВ-

ЛИ" И ПР. ПРОТИВ ЭТА СЕБЯ,ПРОИЗВЕЛА ВПЕЧАТЛЕНИЕ НА ВСЕХ, НИКТО НЕ ДУМАЛ, ЧТО
Я НЕМНОГО УМЕЮ ПЕТЬ. ВСЕ МЫ ОЧЕНЬ ОГОРЧИЛИСЬ, ЧТО НЕ БЫЛО ТЕБЯ, А ОСОБЕННО
ОЧЕНЬ СКОЛЬКО... НЕ ПРИХОДИТ МНЕ ПАМЯТЬ,ТО УЖЕ 7 ОКТЯБРЬСКИХ И 6 НОВЫХ
ГОДОВ... ПРАЗДНИКОВ — ЭТО НЕ ВКЛЮЧАЯ ПРОЧИХ ФАМИЛЬНЫХ ТОРЖЕСТВ Я
ОДНА!!! КАК НЕ СПРАВЕДЛИВА ЖИЗНЬ. Я ВСЕ ПОНИМАЮ,ЧТО ТЫ РАБОТАЕШЬ, И ЧТО ЭТО
ТВОЙ ДОЛГ И ЧТО-ТЫ ЛЮБИШЬ СВОЮ РАБОТУ И ОЧЕНЬ ДОБРОСОВЕСТНО ОТНОСИШЬСЯ КО
ВСЕМУ ЭТОМУ,НО ТЕМ НЕ МЕНЕЕ Я КАК-ТО ЧИСТО ПО-ОБЫВАТЕЛЬСКИ РАССУЖДАЮ (ПО-
ЖЕНСКИ). СТРАДАЮ, СТРАШУСЬ СВОЕГО ОДИНОЧЕСТВА. И ВОТ — ЭТО ВСЕ ОСОБЕННО ПРО-
СЫПАЕТСЯ ВО МНЕ,КОГДА НАСТУПАЮТ КАКИЕ-НИБУДЬ ТОРЖЕСТВА.Я ВСЕГДА РАДУЮСЬ,
КОГДА КОНЧАЕТСЯ ПРАЗДНИК И НАСТУПАЕТ ОБЫЧНЫЙ РАБОЧИЙ ДЕНЬ.Я КАК-ТО СЕБЯ
ЧУВСТВУЮ ИНАЧЕ,КАК БУДТО БЫСТРЕЙ КОНЧАЕТСЯ И НАЧИНАЕТСЯ ДЕНЬ. ДОЕХАЛА Я ХО-
РОШО. ВСЕ БЫЛО ТАК,КАК ТЫ МНЕ ГОВОРИЛ,ТАК ЧТО Я НАПРАСНО ВОЛНОВАЛАСЬ. ВЕРА
ИВА УШЛА ЗА НЕДЕЛЮ ДО ПРАЗДНИКА И СЛОМАЛА НОГУ В ЛАДЫЖКЕ.СЕЙЧАС ОНА В
ГИПСЕ.ВАНЮШКА ИС ПАДАЕТ С НОГ,К ТОМУ ЖЕ ЮРА ЗАБОЛЕЛ ВОСПАЛЕНИЕМ ЛЕГКИХ ВТО-
РИЧНО. ЭТО ВСЕ ИДЕТ НАШЕГО СЫНА (ВСЯКИЕ БЕСКОНЕЧНЫЕ БОЛЕЗНИ). НАДО, ДОРОГОЙ
МОЙ, ПОДУМАТЬ ХОРОШО О ДЕТСКОМ САДЕ?! ТРОЙКИ БОЛЯТ СОВЕРШЕННО НЕ ХВАТАЕТ
... ДО СВИДАНИЯ,ДОРОГОЙ МОЙ И ХОРОШИЙ САМЫЙ ЛЮБИМЫЙ И ВАЖНЫЙ ДЛЯ ЧЕЛОВЕК.
ЦЕЛУЮ ТЕБЯ,ПИШИ МНЕ, КАК СЕБЯ ЧУВСТВУЕШЬ,ПИШИ,ЧТО ЛЮБИШЬ МЕНЯ,МОЖЕТ МНЕ
БУДЕТ ЛЕГЧЕ. Д... ПРОЗА!!! ЕСЛИ ВОЗМОЖНО,ТО Я ТЕБЯ ПРОШУ ДАВАТЬ МНЕ 2500
РУБЛЕЙ В МЕСЯЦ.

6/XI—60г. ЗДРАВСТВУЙ,ДОРОГОЙ ПАПОЧКА! ПОЗДРАВЛЯЮ ТЕБЯ С 43 ГОДОВЩИНОЙ ОК-
ТЯБРЯ! КАК ТЫ СЕБЯ ЧУВСТВУЕШЬ? МЫ ВСЕ ЗДОРОВЫ. ЗАВТРА МЫ ИДЕМ К ТЕТЕ ВЕРЕ.

Hidden bugging equipment

in somewhat Bohemian circles where his occasional absences would not be noticed so much as if he had lived a strict routine life in a suburb.

He was able to paint reasonably well so his cover as an artist was never suspected. More important he utilised the solitude of his studio for radioing his information to Moscow. None knew better than Abel that the frequent use of radio transmissions for espionage was fraught with the risk of discovery. He devised new techniques and codes for tapping out messages at a high speed in a much shorter time than most transmissions would take. Even so he took care to move his transmission headquarters as often as possible.

Even when the sub-agent he mistrusted defected to the Americans in France after being belatedly recalled to Russia, it was a measure of Abel's thoroughness as a spy-master that the Americans had the greatest difficulty in finding him. Abel had never even revealed his cover name to the sub-agent. All the latter could tell the CIA was that he had a place in Brooklyn.

The Russians tipped off Abel that the sub-agent had defected and the former immediately moved to Florida with the aim of crossing into Mexico if he thought the CIA were on his trail. But, as nothing aroused his suspicions that he was being followed, he returned to New York in a few months and checked in at the Hotel Latham under the name of Martin Collins. Here he was finally arrested by the Americans who found 'a block of wood covered with sandpaper – the block came apart and contained a 250-page booklet with a series of numbers, all in five-digit groups, on each page . . . a stubby pencil with an eraser that concealed a cavity was also found; inside the cavity were eighteen micro-films, several of them from Colonel Abel's wife and daughter'.

It is probable that Abel left these things behind deliberately to deceive the CIA. He managed to destroy most incriminating evidence before he was taken away.

The Abel case, however, revealed the extent to which Russian spies use what are called 'drops' or 'letter-boxes' (*dubok* is the Russian name for these secret hiding-places for messages). The sub-agent told the Americans that he had been using a hole in a flight of steps in Prospect Park in Brooklyn for messages. Park workers had noticed the hole and filled it in with cement. The FBI went to the Park, opened up the hole and found inside a message in a hollowed-out bolt. This read:

'Nobody came meeting either 8th or 9th
at 203.2030 as I was advised he should.
Why? Should he be inside or outside?
Is time wrong? Place seems right. Please check.'

A hole in a flight of steps: somewhere to leave secret messages

This message illustrates how dissatisfied Abel had become with his sub-agent who seems to have been neglectful about picking up messages.

Briefing for a spy, complete with spelling mistakes from a Russian employer

It was proved afterwards that this message had been typed out on Abel's own typewriter, a fact which helped to convict him. It is curious that so efficient an agent as Abel should have used as a 'drop' a hole which was likely to be filled up. Yet one of the recurring weaknesses of the Soviet espionage system in the 'fifties was the highly unsatisfactory hiding-places chosen by agents for leaving messages. A crack in a wooden fence was sometimes used and even a split in a railway sleeper where maintenance parties were working regularly.

The answer to this may be that Russian children do not play games of leaving secret messages for friends in similar type hiding-places as do children in many Western countries. And the 'drops' the Russians use are frequently the kind of hiding-places utilised by children. And so Abel was charged with transmitting military information to the Soviet Union. On 23 October, 1957, he was sentenced to thirty years' imprisonment.

Luckily for him he only served a few years of his sentence. He was, without question, a spy of vital importance to Russia and when, three years later, the Russians captured the US flier Gary Powers, who had been shot down in his U-2 aircraft, the Soviet Union knew the moment they sentenced Powers to ten years' imprisonment that they could bargain with the Americans. In due course Powers was exchanged for Abel.

Infiltration and disinformation: these are the two techniques in which Soviet Russia has perfected her espionage. Let us take the use of infiltration first. It has led to some blunders and the Soviet Union's losses in spies probably outnumber those of any other power. On the other hand it is a measure of the extent to which they do spy. Taken more seriously, one could say that for every ten caught possibly another thirty succeed. The ratio could be higher than that.

The Russians, like all totalitarian states, where sheer fear of the consequences of failure may force men to betray their country, suffer greatly from defectors. Much of America's intelligence has come from defectors from inside the KGB. But again this poses its risks. Some at least of these defectors are deliberately planted by the KGB to feed false information to the country to which they defect.

Usually, to disarm the suspicious interrogators of whichever Western nation they have chosen for sanctuary, these defectors bring with them some sensational and true intelligence. Sometimes, but not always, this involves naming a Western spy who has turned over to the Soviet Union. The Russians are careful to select someone who is already safely in their custody, or one who is already of no further use to them. The object is to make mischief between Allies. Thus if a Russian defects to the Americans, he will name someone in

II. URGENT CALL

case you urgently need to meet me you are
place an announcement in "The Daily Telegraph,"
sect on "PERSONAL", which would read as follows:
"Many thanks to all my friends visiting
our Wedding. Barbara"

--- ------------- -----"

n suterday of this week the announsment is published I
weel be seeing you near "Pinner Parish Church" at I4-00
hrs or I5-00 hrs/ Example: an announsment is published
on any day of the week- I shall see you on the comming
Saterday./

You letter to the above newspaper and a postal-
order for an amount in question/ about 40/-/ we recommend you to send from another town about
100 miles from the place you live.
The letter is to be written [on the writing machine] ~~with a changed handwriting~~.

In case I urgently need to see you I'll send (to address→
You a ~~post-card~~ [Radio-magazine] signed "----------". This would mean that
I'll be waiting for you near "Pinner Perish Church" at
14-00 hrs or I5-00 hrs on Saterday of the week the postcard is send.

address

Rudolf Nureyev, world famous ballet dancer, dances with Margot Fonteyn at Covent Garden

Natalia Makarova and Yuri Soloviev with the Kirov Ballet. This photograph was taken three days before she defected

the British, French or Italian Secret Services who is working for the Soviet Union. And if he defects to the British, he will probably name an American.

By this means the Russians set out to create mistrust between Allies and to destroy morale. During President Kennedy's term of office the Russians skilfully employed bogus defectors to convince the United States that the French Secret Service had been infiltrated by the Russians and was totally discredited. This even led to President Kennedy sending a secret message of warning to General de Gaulle, which, far from being appreciated, was regarded as an insult to France.

Thus disinformation is often used with infiltration, though apart from this the Soviet Secret Service puts out a mass of false rumours and carefully planted disinformation to mislead other Secret Services. In the early days this was somewhat

crudely done: today it is frequently managed so cunningly that it is not always possible to interpret the motives behind it.

One of the subtler forms of infiltration practised by the Soviet Union is the sending of agents to join the priesthood or other Church bodies. This has been done on a relatively small scale, but it is known that one Russian youth who had been brought up in the Orthodox Russian Church was sent to Italy at the age of fifteen with orders to take instruction in the Roman Catholic Church on the understanding that if he was accepted into the priesthood eventually, he would become a Soviet agent.

One of his earliest assignments as a priest was to go out to Latin America to find sub-agents there. He did more than this: he organised an association of Marxist priests in Guatemala. A number of Church organisations, not all of them Catholic, have been infiltrated by Soviet agents, and often liberal-minded and radical non-Communist priests are exploited in the Russian cause. In the Middle East Russian agents have entered the Greek Orthodox Church under the guise of priests and monks.

The audacity of the Russians in worming their way into places and institutions where one could hardly believe a spy could exist for long is unparalleled. It requires patience of a special kind, certainly courage, and above all the ability to play an unnatural role over many years. It becomes even more daring when they take the risk of using the nationals of another country to achieve this sort of thing. Who would have expected the Russians to try to recruit men such as Donald Maclean, son of a former British Cabinet Minister, Cambridge-educated and a member of the British Foreign Office? Or 'Kim' Philby, son of a knight and actually head of the Russian section of the British Secret Service? Or of Georges Paques, member of the French national defence staff and later deputy press chief at NATO headquarters?

Yet each one of these men was won over to the Soviet cause and served it while still appearing to be a loyal and key official in his own country. Paques, it is true, was eventually caught and sentenced to life imprisonment in 1964, but he had already been giving the Russians vital information since 1944. But Maclean and Philby both escaped in time to take refuge in the Soviet Union where they are still living.

Chapter 9

The escape racket

A good spy, like a good prisoner-of-war, is always expected to try to escape when he is captured. But his chances of doing this are considerably less than those of a prisoner-of-war who usually has some freedom of movement and, being together with fellow-countrymen, has the opportunity of being helped to escape.

The spy, once caught, is usually kept in a top security jail and is guarded day and night. He is not allowed to have any visitors. And a modern top security prison is almost foolproof against escape attempts.

The moment a spy is caught the country which employs him is in a quandary. It needs to have its spy safely back home so that he can be 'de-briefed', as they call it. This means intensive questioning of the returned agent, finding out what information he still possessed when he was caught and unable to pass on, learning exactly what he told his captors and, most important of all, discovering to what extent his own spy network and fellow-agents have been endangered.

At the same time the masters of the spy who has 'come in from the cold' want to make quite sure that he has not been blackmailed by his captors to work for them. However sure they may be of one of their most trusted men, it is essential that they take into account the chances of this, however slight.

Meanwhile the nation employing the spy held in captivity has to pretend that it knew nothing about his activities and to disown him as a spy. A cat-and-mouse game is played at diplomatic level between the spy's country and that of his captors. Appeals are made for leniency and an early release from prison. Usually they are met with a chilly refusal.

The object of the captor country is to hold the spy until such time that, whatever information he has to pass back to his masters, it is totally useless. For example, they will try to

**Gerald Brooke. He spent
four years in a Russian Jail**

interrogate him until they learn more details of his network. They will also try to round up the rest of that network before releasing the spy.

At a certain stage in these protracted proceedings some bargaining may be done. If he is a very important agent, the spy's government may offer to surrender an agent they hold in prison in exchange for the release of one of their men. It all depends whether the other side desperately want their man back.

The Russians are past-masters at this game. Probably more than any other nation they believe in rescuing their spies when the latter are caught. Their aim, therefore, is always to have a certain number of foreigners in jail whom they can at the appropriate moment use as bargaining counters. Sometimes these foreigners are really spies, like Gary Powers when he was exchanged for Rudolf Abel. More often than

A spy is apprehended

not they are merely indiscreet visitors who have allowed themselves to be trapped into some offence, or simply clumsy, somewhat amateur agents.

Obviously when the bargaining pawns held by the Russians are from the espionage point of view people of little value, exchange deals are more difficult to bring about. Then the Russians employ another technique. It usually takes two forms; probably each is used simultaneously. The first is to put out a report that the person they hold in jail is in poor health and that on humanitarian grounds an exchange of prisoners would be just. The other method is for the wife of the spy they want back to write a sympathetic letter to the parents, wife or other relative of the man they hold in jail, suggesting she should put pressure on her government for an exchange deal.

In Britain these tactics have often succeeded. The Government of the day at first stands firm and proclaims that it cannot exchange a convicted spy for one of their own nationals. Then questions are asked in the House of Commons, usually raising the question of the need for a compassionate approach to the suggested exchange. The issue is brought up in the newspapers and, finally and reluctantly, a deal is agreed upon.

Thus a democratic country is at a permanent disadvantage in dealing with a totalitarian state. The latter does not have to worry about public opinion or the press, or Parliamentary questions. They can – and they do – find excuses for arresting foreigners on trumped up charges in order always to have bargaining counters. If a Soviet spy is captured in a Western country, the probability is that shortly afterwards a citizen of that country will be arrested in Russia. He may have been lured into a black market deal, or he may have simply taken photographs of the Kremlin: it is simple for the KGB to concoct a charge.

Emigres fleeing Russia after the Revolution

Sometimes, of course, exchange negotiations break down. Then the only hope is of a carefully planned escape for the captured spy.

To escape from Russia, once one is actually inside a jail, is well nigh impossible. Indeed to escape from that country at all when one is free, but on the run, is extremely difficult. The best organised escape route from Russia was that set up by the British during the Civil War of 1917-22 when Paul Dukes was head of the British Secret Service in Russia.

Dukes had gone to Russia in 1909 to study music and was given the task of investigating the revolutionary underworld. After the revolution he relied on his skill at disguising himself to keep him all the time one step ahead of the Cheka who had put a high price on his head. The disguises he used would have done credit to any professional actor. He posed sometimes as Comrade Piotrovsky, agent of the Cheka with a

Sir Paul Dukes, in four disguises

Russian passport which stated this; on other occasions he was a cripple, a Red Army soldier, a bearded proletarian and a consumptive intellectual.

The absolute hell of being permanently on the run is exemplified in what he wrote afterwards: 'I was isolated, with a large quantity of information accumulating, part of which I was obliged to destroy. I continued to keep up communication . . . through the medium of an officer who was employed at the Admiralty. As he considered it unsafe to meet in private houses we met in parks or public places, arranging our rendezvous by means of dropping notes into one of a series of little holes – designated originally for flags – in the parapet of the Neva . . . Towards the end of April I found a note in the parapet hole saying that "the fruit was ripening" and that a "postman" – that is a courier – might shortly be available.'

In this period high-speed Royal Navy coastal motor-boats were used to establish contacts with British agents in Russia and Finland and also to rescue them. Often these craft had to contend with fire from shore batteries and Lieutenant W S Agar was awarded the VC for the role he played in these activities. It is also worth mentioning that Paul Dukes was knighted when he finally escaped back to England.

The classic example of the carefully organised escape of a spy from prison in modern times is that of George Blake, who got away from Wormwood Scrubs Jail in London and found his way to Russia.

Blake, the son of an Egyptian Jew married to a Dutchwoman, joined the Dutch Resistance movement as a youth during the German occupation of Holland in World War II. He escaped to Britain, joined the Royal Navy as an ordinary seaman and eventually became an officer. His

George Blake, sentenced to 42 years imprisonment in 1961

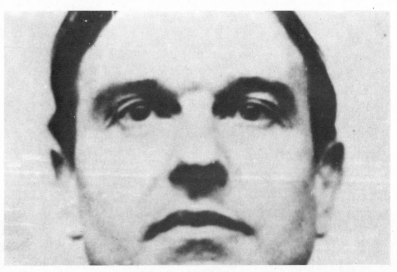

knowledge of languages impressed the authorities and he was later employed on intelligence work. After the war he became a senior agent of the British Secret Service in Germany.

In 1948 he was appointed as a vice-consul in Korea, but still continued with his work as an agent, which was unusual because the general rule is that a member of the Diplomatic Service does not mix in espionage.

Then, for three years, Blake was interned by the North Koreans and subjected to brain-washing. On his release from captivity when the Korean War ended in 1953, Blake rejoined the British Secret Service and was sent to Berlin with instructions to infiltrate the Soviet network and to pose as a double-agent.

There is still an element of mystery about Blake's next moves. To play the highly dangerous game of a double-agent even in the cause of one's own country (Blake was a British subject because his father had a British passport) is fraught with grave risks for any spy. Effectively to pose as a double-agent one must pass on at least some useful information to the enemy. At some point or other the question is bound to arise: is he telling the enemy too much?

The charge against Blake ultimately was that he had passed on too much information to the Russians and that he had not merely posed as a Soviet agent, but actually joined their ranks. A German informer warned the British Secret Service that their man in Berlin had betrayed several Western agents, both British and American, to the Russians and consequently sent some of them to their death.

Blake was told by the British Foreign Office to report to London. When he did so he was arrested and in May, 1961, sentenced to 42 years' imprisonment for betraying secrets to the Russians. Astonishingly, Blake admitted the charges, made no excuse for his conduct and actually pleaded guilty. What is more he stated at his trial that he had decided 'to join the Communist side to establish a balanced and more just society'.

No doubt the Russians made various attempts to have Blake exchanged for one of their prisoners. Such a plan was almost certainly rejected by the British on the grounds that his release would further endanger their networks. Somehow the information that an exchange was ruled out, but that an attempt at a rescue would be made was passed to Blake in prison.

Late on Saturday night, 22 October, 1966, it was announced that George Blake had escaped from Wormwood Scrubs Prison. A nation-wide alert operation was set in motion and a watch kept at all British airports. Yet at this very moment Blake was hiding out in an apartment only a short distance from the prison. A few months later he was in Moscow.

The secret of Blake's escape and how it was organised has

George Blake, the moment he set foot in Britain after being held by the Communists in Korea

Sean Bourke. He helped Blake to escape from Wormwood Scrubs

been carefully kept. Neither the Russians, nor the British will tell exactly what happened. But it is clear that the KGB went to great lengths to plan this operation over a long period.

One interesting fact emerged which suggested the British had been singularly careless in their security arrangements: for a short period Blake and Konon Molody were in the same prison. It is possible, therefore, that they could have communicated with one another.

The key man in Blake's escape, on his own admission, was Sean Bourke, an Irishman who had been a fellow-prisoner in Wormwood Scrubs. Bourke has since asserted that Blake asked him to help in his rescue and that the whole affair was done solely on his own initiative.

When Bourke was released from prison he started to plan the escape operation. Miniature radio equipment was smuggled into Blake at Wormwood Scrubs so that he was able to talk to Bourke by radio. Nobody appears to have monitored those conversations.

Bourke himself operated his radio at a site quite close to the prison walls. Every detail of the escape plan was passed by radio so that, when the moment arrived, Blake was able to take full advantage of all the local knowledge of movements of prison officers.

At 5.30 pm on the night of his escape Blake was watching television with other prisoners. He left the room and told two prison officers he was going back to his cell to read. Instead he went up to the landing on the second floor to a window, of which he had already loosened one of the bars. It is now thought that he had already broken the bar, then replaced it and held it in position with some adhesive tape blackened by boot polish.

Blake got through the window, lowered himself on to the roof of a covered passage below and had only a drop of about five feet to the ground. It was now six o'clock and raining fairly steadily. Timing the movements of the prison officers who patrolled the walls of the jail, Blake made his way to the wall where on the inside a rope ladder had already been thrown over by Bourke.

In a matter of minutes Blake was over the wall, jumping the twenty feet to the ground where Bourke was waiting with a car in the roadway. This was the worst part of the escape and Bourke said afterwards, when interviewed in a television programme, that Blake 'knocked himself unconscious when he jumped and badly twisted his wrist'.

Bourke dragged Blake into the car and drove off to the nearby apartment where he was to lie low until the hue and cry for him had ceased.

After Blake's escape to Russia Bourke joined him over there. But Bourke was no starry-eyed admirer of the Soviet regime and he found that, now the escape had been

The first picture from inside Russia of George Blake. He is with his 71 year old mother

successfully negotiated, neither Blake nor the KGB had any use for him. He was regarded as somewhat of a nuisance. So Bourke went back to Ireland where he was immediately faced with extradition proceedings with a view to his being sent back to Britain to be charged with aiding Blake's escape.

When the case was heard Bourke declared: 'I have never been a Communist . . . I sprang Blake from a slow, lingering death', meaning that he did this on humanitarian grounds and not because of ideological sympathies. Ordered to be extradited, he appealed against this decision and won his case. Thus it is that the only detailed account we have of Blake's escape is that of Sean Bourke himself.

Bargaining in spy exchanges became a minor industry in Berlin during the 'Cold War'. Originally it was simply an exchange traffic in minor agents and rarely had any publicity in the newspapers.

Sometimes an American or Briton would accidentally cross the border into East Berlin. Immediately he would be arrested and an attempt made to exchange him for a minor Soviet agent held by the Allied powers. Occasionally the Russians would kidnap a Westerner and hold him in East Berlin until they could persuade the Allied authorities to make an exchange.

In self defence, the Americans or British would sometimes hit back by kidnapping a Russian to force the exchange of a man they desperately needed to get back. Then, as the 'Cold War' became less tense, this gangster-style bartering was succeeded by more diplomatic approaches. In recent years a certain lawyer in East Germany has been the chief intermediary in arranging exchanges of agents. Astonishingly, he has managed to win the confidence of both sides.

The Russians never let up for a moment in their campaign

Greville Wynne. After spending eleven months in a Russian jail, he was exchanged for Gordon Lonsdale

PIX NR 14 MALTA 330 1145/26 T/A APPHO LONDON 333 THE FORMER BRITISH SPY GREVILLE WYNNE ABOUT TO ENTER HIS RESIDENCE AT MSIDA YACHT MARINA MALTA   PARDISON.

for the release of Konon Molody, who had been arrested in London under his cover name of Gordon Lonsdale and sentenced to 25 years' imprisonment. Equally they fought hard for the release of Peter and Helen Kroger, who were part of the Molody network and had been sent to prison for 20 years.

Molody was eventually exchanged for Greville Wynne, a British business man who had been arrested on the grounds that he had been associated with Penkovsky, a traitor in the Russian ranks. It is significant of the faith which Russian agents have in their masters that Molody was convinced the whole time he was in prison that he would be exchanged for another prisoner or that the KGB would fix his rescue.

The coolness of Molody in prison was remarkable. He continued to deny that his real name was Molody, he played chess and translated three books – all, incidentally, on the subject of espionage – into Russian. When released from prison he even had the cheek to ask for the translations to be sent on to him in Russia. It is not known if this request was granted.

The Krogers were that rare combination in espionage – a highly successful man and wife team. They had been top Russian agents for many years. Their real names were Morris and Lona Cohen. When there was a big round-up of Soviet agents in the USA in the late 'forties, the Cohens left America for New Zealand, where they adopted the names of Peter and Helen Kroger. Later they travelled to Britain, set up a second-hand bookshop in the Strand in London and became a vital part of Molody's network.

In their bungalow at Ruislip in Middlesex they established a communications centre with Moscow. After their arrest the police found in the bungalow radio transmission equipment,

Peter and Helen Kroger on their way to Warsaw, after their release

Hidden transmitters behind a radiogram; travellers cheques in the loft. Some of the evidence against the Krogers found in their bungalow

The Kroger's bungalow in Ruislip

cameras hidden in the loft and a microdot-reader in a secret compartment of a tin of talcum powder.

When the Russians eventually arranged for the release of the Krogers they had by far the best of the bargain. The Soviet Union got back two of their most trusted agents in exchange for Gerald Brooke, a young British lecturer who was not even a spy, but had merely been foolish enough to try to distribute anti-Communist leaflets inside Russia.

Chapter 10

Codes are always changing

Codes and ciphers preceded languages in that they were the first attempt at conveying meanings and messages in written form. As these heiroglyphics, often carved on stone, were known only to the privileged few, it could be said that the first languages were really secret communications.

The earliest known form of language was a combination of pictures, intended to depict actions, and symbols to convey link signs such as verbs in the text. It was many years before any European succeeded in correctly de-ciphering some of the ancient Egyptian hieroglyphics.

One of the earliest known codes was the 'Julius Caesar Cipher', used for secret messages by Caesar when he sent messages from Gaul back to Rome. His method was quite simple: he substituted a letter four places later in the alphabet for each letter in his actual message. Thus the phrase *His rebus factis* would become in cipher MNV UHEZV IDFXNV, allowing for the fact that the Latin alphabet lacks the letters J, K, W and Y.

Some of the earliest authorities on cryptography were scholars of the Roman Catholic Church, notably Abbot Trithemius who wrote a book on the subject in Holland. He also invented the system of encipherment, the basis of which is again substitution, but instead of substituting one letter for another as in the case of the Caesar Cipher, he gave each letter in the alphabet a series of twenty phrases, the use of any one of which denoted that letter in the code. Obviously this was a more difficult code to break, but it was also cumbersome and took a long time to compose the messages. The reason for the choice of twenty phrases was so that sense could be made out of the actual code. For example, if one wished to write the word cab in code a suitable selection of phrases for c, a and b would be 'Lovely – Mary – you are admired'.

It is not a code for anyone in a hurry to pass on information.

The Rosetta Stone. This was the clue to the decipherment of ancient Egyptian writing

155

Francis Bacon 1561-1626

Roger Bacon in the thirteenth century investigated some of the ancient mystic codes, but his writings were considered heretical and he was imprisoned. His namesake, Francis Bacon, invented the Bilateral Cipher, a somewhat complicated system which involved the printer or writer using some letters in Roman and others in Italic. The idea of this was that the actual text of the message made sense and did not seem like a code. It was only when the variations of the lettering were considered that the hidden meaning was revealed to those who knew the key.

Bacon's system was still being used in Russia in the nineteenth century.

During the English Civil War of the seventeenth century Sir John Trevanion was imprisoned in Colchester Castle as a Royalist sympathiser. One day a letter was sent to him. It seemed straightforward and innocuous enough, as it was only a message of sympathy. The prison governor passed it on to his prisoner. Sir John read the letter and then asked that evening if he could go to the chapel to pray.

The request was granted and he was left alone there. When he did not re-appear the jailers went in to see what had happened. Their prisoner had flown. The clue lay in a re-examination of the letter. Taking the third letter after each punctuation mark, the hidden message read: 'Panel at east end of chapel slides.'

The French were foremost in the cryptographical field in the seventeenth and eighteenth centuries. They came to grief when Napoleon tried not only to simplify but to speed up cipher composition. His Great Cipher had less than 200 signs, its basis being the assignment of numbers to letters and in some cases numbers for names. But Napoleon's generals, who were the only people who knew about the Cipher, were not very imaginative in their use of it.

Colchester Castle as it is today

In fact they used it so clumsily that the Emperor Alexander of Russia was able afterwards to tell the French: 'We always knew your plans because whenever we captured your secret dispatches we had no difficulty in deciphering them.'

Ciphers and codes came to be used in the United States during the Civil War when General McClellan, head of the Ohio troops, and Alan Pinkerton, then Federal Intelligence chief, with the aid of a telegraphic expert, composed a new cipher based on word transposition.

Spies frequently captured stations where cipher messages were on a file, but they failed to decipher a single one of them. To test the reliability of their messages the Cipher Department from time to time published in the newspapers copies of captured telegrams, asking for anyone who could decipher them to report back.

Allan Pinkerton. Private Detective and Director of Intelligence to Lincoln

Nobody ever did. The cipher team always kept a step ahead by making slight changes in code words and route patterns.

When, in 1864, the French had established Maximilian as Emperor of Mexico, the American Government ordered troops to the Texas border. The Secretary of State, William H. Seward, wanted to send a message to Paris which would serve as a diplomatic warning that the US would take further action if the French did not evacuate from Mexico. To send such a message in the clear would exacerbate the situation and probably provoke a war, so Seward decided it must go in code. So he used the numerical American diplomatic code which had not been operated for many years.

The message went off by cable in about 1,100 groups of three, four and five figure characters. Eventually the State Department got a bill from the cable company for 23,000 dollars. Seward was furious and demanded to know why such an extortionate charge had been made. The reply was that to discourage further coded messages of this type the company had decided to double their normal charges and that each number was charged for separately. Thus if a message read '634 – 21052 – 6790' the charge would not be for three words, but for 12 numbers. And the total number of figures in the text was 4,600.

Never again did the State Department use this code in their cables.

It was in the 1880's that cryptography underwent a complete revolution and all the major powers were fighting one another to produce safer ciphers and, at the same time, trying to break those of their adversaries.

In the Boer War the British used Latin as a cipher, which proved effective as the Boers had never been taught this subject at school. But the man who is first credited with having pointed the way to Latin as a code form was Sir Charles Napier, the British Commander in India at the siege of Sindh. He wired the shortest cipher message on record:

'PECCAVI'.

Translated, this read in English: 'I have sinned.' An alert Intelligence officer the other end was intended to deduce from this that Napier had captured Sindh.

World War I saw battles won and lost through effective or blundering use of codes and ciphers. Early in that war, when radio communications were still in their infancy, the messages sent out by German, French, British and Russians were all lost in total confusion because each was jamming the others. On another occasion two Russian generals on the eastern front had mislaid their cipher codes and they had to communicate with each other in plain language with the result that the Germans intercepted the messages and were

Sir Charles Napier

able to change their movements accordingly. The Russians suffered a terrible defeat.

Spies in World War I often used very simple, innocuous phrases for sending coded messages. One day a naval censor read an ordinary domestic cable from someone in London to a relative in Holland stating quite simply: 'Mother is dead'. It seemed straightforward enough, but intuition prompted the censor to alter 'dead' to 'deceased' before he let the message through.

Back came a reply, which was also intercepted: 'Is mother dead or deceased?' Now the censor was really worried. He automatically suspected all messages to Holland because it was known that German agents in Britain passed information back to Germany via addresses in Holland. The fact that the recipient of the cable had queried the changing of a single word even though its meaning was to all intents and purposes the same convinced him it must be a code. And so it proved to be when, shortly afterwards, the sender of the cable was arrested.

The first telegram before it was altered

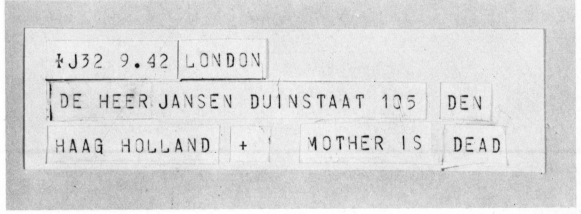

The second telegram This one gave the game away

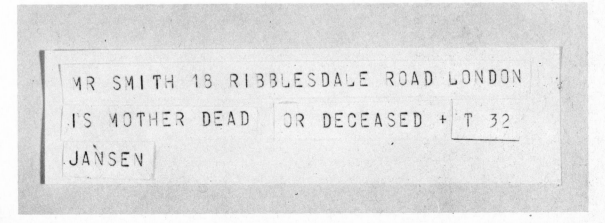

An example of the microdot process

MIDDLE (OF) DECEMBER AIRPLANE PARTS AND MA-
CHINERY FROM DOUGLAS AND LOCKHEED IN NEW
ORLEANS AND GALVESTON ARE TO BE SHIPPED FOR
CASABLANCA AND RABAT. THE NAMED FIRMS INTEND
TO BUILD THERE ONE ASSEMBLY PLANT EACH IN
ORDER TO TAKE UP LATER TOTAL PRODUCTION
BY MAKING USE OF AFRICA'S RAW MATERIALS. THE
SHIPMENT WILL TAKE PLACE ON FORMER DELTA
LINERS. THREE HUNDRED TECHNICIANS OF EACH
FIRM ARE GOING ALONG. THE SHIPS WILL BE AT-
TACHED TO CONVOY. TECHNICAL VANGUARD HAS
ALREADY DEPARTED BY WAY OF PAN-AMERICAN
AIRLINES. (I) REPEAT THE NAMES: NEW ORLEANS,
GALVESTON, DOUGLAS, LOCKHEED, CASABLANCA,
RABAT.

Agent's Code Book

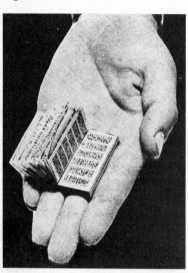

Today much subtler means of communication are employed by professionals in the espionage game. By far the most effective of these is the microdot system.

The microdot is a tiny piece of film that must be magnified to several times its size before it can be read. Microdot photography can reproduce a whole document on a particle of film that is so small that it just about covers a single full-stop in a sentence. Quite often it is delicately glued on to a typewritten letter which can be sent through normal airmail without attracting any attention.

In fact the microdot communication is now superseding even coded, secret radio transmission in the espionage game. Modern methods of detection make it exceedingly difficult for an agent to pass on messages of any length over a long period without being found out. Codes and ciphers are, however, employed even in microdot correspondence.

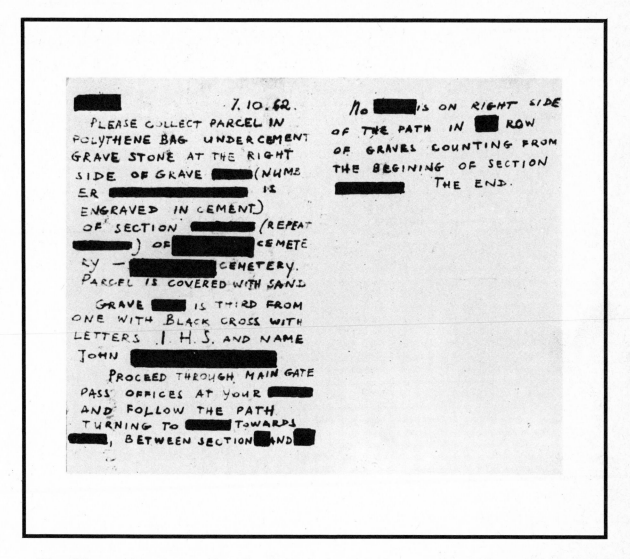

**A developed secret message
written in an ordinary
looking letter**

The difference between a code and a cipher is that the former is based on symbols or groups of letters to indicate whole words while ciphers use single letters or pairs of letters or numbers as substitutes for single letters. The disadvantage of codes is that those using them need to possess code books which not only take up a lot of room, but cannot easily be destroyed in an emergency.

The Russians have developed the technique of ciphers to a highly sophisticated degree. Most ciphers, once they have been carefully analysed and broken down, can be deciphered today by the code and cipher computers which most of the great powers employ in their Intelligence headquarters. The most effective of these code-breaking computers is that in the US National Security Agency at Fort Meade in Maryland. But the new methods introduced by the Russians make their own ciphers almost one hundred per cent foolproof.

The equipment of a spy.
Codes, notebooks,
instructions from using
them and radio broadcast
procedure. Penkovsky, the
man who used them was
arrested by the Russians
for spying

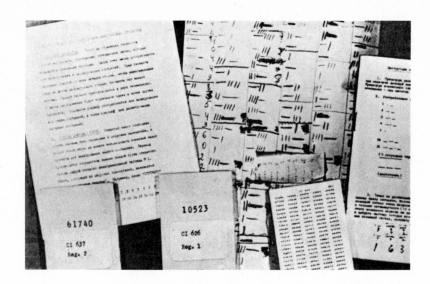

As a safeguard Soviet agents who are trusted sufficiently
to be given cipher information have a cipher pad which is
really a miniature book about the size of a postage stamp and
printed on nitrated cellulose so that with the touch of a match
or lighter flame it can be burnt instantaneously.

A vital clue on Russian cipher and code methods was
obtained some few years ago when American code-crackers
secured a microdot film that had been secreted in the cover of
a book-matches pack. This revealed that one of the tricks of
Russian cipher composition at that time was the use of what is
known as modular arithmetic. This means that whether in
adding or subtracting in columns the numbers are neither
carried over nor deducted from the next column.

Thus, if you add

$$5,703$$
$$4,806$$

the true total is 10,509.

But by modular arithmetic the answer would be 9,509.

To baffle any would-be computer analysts the 'modular'
answer and not the true total would be used in a cipher text.

Cryptography will undoubtedly continue to change
probably at a faster rate than in the past because now there is
the challenge of computers to compete with. Both in the CIA
and in the KGB top agents have training in advanced
mathematics in so far as they can be related to cryptography.

Sometimes the fact that codes and ciphers can swiftly be
broken is turned to advantage by planting false information in
what seems to be a current code or cipher and allowing it to be
captured. On more than one occasion such 'disinformation'
had caused rifts between friendly powers and resulted in the
suspension of a key agent because he has been falsely named as
a traitor.

Opposite:
Thumbscrews
The Iron Collar

Chapter 11

Tortures and interrogations

It is not so much getting caught which is the dread of every spy, it is the knowledge that in many cases capture means interrogation and failure to give the required answers can mean torture.

In ancient times confessions were forced from spies by use of the rack, the turnscrew and trussing up a prisoner over a slow fire. As a rule only the most zealous of religious martyrs, depending on the fanatical strength they drew from their faith and beliefs, were able to remain silent under such horrors. It is not surprising that such men and women were later made saints: they deserved to be.

By the end of the eighteenth century the attitude to the interrogation of spies had changed considerably in most civilised countries. This was due not so much to public opinion being revolted by the practice of torture as to the realisation that when this method did not produce a confession and the spy died as a result of injuries inflicted nothing was achieved.

There was also the fact that those who did not die became such raving lunatics that they were incapable of giving any information.

From then on subtler methods of interrogation were applied and torture methods were less drastic but still beastly enough. The aim from then on was to keep the spy alive and ensure that he remained sane in the hope that eventually he would confess.

The Russians in the early years of their communist revolution and the Germans in the Nazi era revived much of the brutality of medieval times. Instead of the rack there was the removal of toe and finger-nails, systematic beatings, perhaps a broken bone or two. But if that failed to make the spy talk, he was taken back to his cell and left alone for a few days. Then the same performance was repeated.

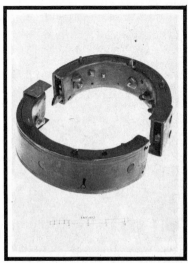

Sometimes the treatment was varied: the victim would simply be kept without sleep for nights on end by jailers who directed blazing lights down on to his face and woke him up every time he dozed off. Often such treatment worked more effectively than physical torture.

Not all the interrogators and torturers were German. One of the worst was a French collaborator named Georges Delfanne, who invented the ordeal of plunging the victim into a bath of ice-cold water, holding him or her down almost to drowning point, and then offering to stop in return for information.

Jean Mulin, one of the most brilliant spies in the ranks of the French Resistance, fell into the hands of incredibly sadistic and stupid interrogators. He was beaten so brutally that he died before he had any chance to confess, though it is unlikely he would have done so had he lived.

During World War II and indeed during the 'Cold War' spies on both sides were often given tiny capsules of cyanide or some other swift-acting, deadly poison which they could swallow on being captured to avoid either being tortured or being forced to confess.

There are, nevertheless, objections to this kind of protective equipment being given to spies. It is defeatist in that it means, if used, an agent's life is lost – possibly unnecessarily, as torture is not always applied. At the same time it tends to alert the captors to the fact that the spy has valuable information. Thus, if he is caught before he has had a chance to swallow the capsule, he is certain to be interrogated very thoroughly.

Some of the ace agents in World War II, both male and female, survived despite being tortured. One was Wing-Commander Forest Frederick Yeo-Thomas, a British spy operating in Occupied France under the code-name of 'Shelley'. Yeo-Thomas had lived in France before the war, working as a director of the fashion house of Molyneux.

Interrogation during the inquisition

A sight dreaded by agents during World War II

He was one of the bravest and most effective agents the British put into the field. Parachuted into France on a number of occasions, he had many lucky escapes before he was finally trapped by the enemy. Once, surrounded by German soldiers and Gestapo agents, he hid himself under a pile of wreaths on a hearse and was driven to safety. 'All the time I lay under those flowers I had a Sten-gun in my hands, ready to fire if necessary,' said Thomas afterwards.

In the end he was betrayed by another agent who had been ruthlessly interrogated by the Germans. Having been instructed to make a rendezvous at a Paris Metro station, he walked straight into the arms of the Gestapo. He was subjected to appalling tortures which left their mark until the end of his days. His refusal to give the Germans any information and his escape from Buchenwald concentration camp resulted in his being awarded the Military Cross and George Medal for 'exceptional gallantry'.

In more recent times spy interrogators have experimented with less drastic but more effective methods of forcing spies to talk. One such is the use of shock therapy, generally known as ECT, or electro-convulsive-therapy. It consists of putting the person to be interrogated to sleep with an injection and then applying mild electric shocks to the brain.

When the spy wakes up he is questioned before the full effects of ECT have worn off. But it was soon found that this was very much a hit-and-miss technique, working quite well with some, but failing to produce the desired results in others. ECT confuses the mind to some extent and quite often obliterates any recollection of recent events from the mind of the victim. ECT is not used on spies today except when they are suffering from acute depression or chronic sleeplessness. In these circumstances, by curing the depression and relaxing a prisoner, he can sometimes be induced to talk.

How Yeo-Thomas escaped

Electric-shock treatment – the application of electric current to various parts of the anatomy, usually the genitals or some nerve centre, is operated by some interrogators with cruel and often successful results.

Various 'truth drugs' have been experimented with and spies are now warned beforehand of the risks involved by such brain-washing. Some of the drugs are injected intravenously and are relatively harmless: their effect is to make the prisoner pleasantly drowsy with something of the feeling of being tipsy but without a hangover. The tongue is loosened and he begins to talk compulsively unless his training and will-power are such as to enable him to resist.

But stepping up the treatment of injecting these 'truth drugs' by giving stronger doses over a long period can, if the man fails to talk, reduce him to a gibbering idiot. He is then of no use to his captors.

Sean Connery about to be interrogated by Gold Finger

Training is now given to spies in how to recognise such brain-washing techniques and to try to withstand their effects. Most spies are given a carefully prepared story to tell to their captors, one that will permit the giving of a certain amount of true information which will not endanger the spy's network, but also a certain amount of false information, usually of a kind which the captors cannot easily disprove. In this way interrogation becomes a prolonged game played by both sides.

The ordeal goes somewhat like this: first the captured spy is questioned and he refuses to answer. An attempt may then be made to give him an injection. He resists the effects of this as best he can and then, after a suitable interval, gives answers to questions, hesitantly at first, so as not to be suspected of talking too easily. Eventually he tells all that has been agreed in the prepared statement.

He then feigns exhaustion and is left alone. The object

Michael Caine being lead to yet another interrogation

here is to avoid further cross-examination too soon. Later, perhaps days later, the captors will return to the questioning. In the meantime they will have gone through their files to see if they can catch him out on any detail. Or they may delay further interrogation for weeks while checks are made.

The whole affair becomes a battle of wits.

There are, of course, many interrogations which are carried out under a pretence of friendliness and hospitality. This is the case when a suspect is invited to come along for an interview, something which is practised by all espionage and counter-espionage services.

Such an interview may take place when some person may have been overheard denouncing someone as a spy, or speaking indiscreetly about matters which in the normal course of events he should know nothing about. Then the questioners want to know why A thinks B is a spy or how A found out about Y. The counter-espionage service will invite such people to call at their offices. Sometimes they will not respond and, in a democracy, it is not always easy to compel them to do so. But more often than not, for a variety of reasons, they will comply, out of fear, or even because they are flattered to be asked to co-operate.

There is, however, the occasion when an actual member of a Secret Service may be suspected of treachery and he is asked to explain matters. 'Kim' Philby, the Soviet spy who worked for years as a member of the British Secret Service, once found himself in this position. He was summoned to call at the offices of MI5, the counter-espionage service.

Philby, of course, knew he was guilty, but also realised that his British masters were not sure about this. He has given his own account of this particular interrogation:

'I offered to put a summary of what I had said on paper. It was possible that our talk was bugged, and I wanted a written record to correct any bias that the microphone might have betrayed. When I went back for my second interrogation a few days later, White* gave my note a cursory glance, then edged towards the real focus of his interest. We might clarify matters, he said, if I gave him an account of my relations with Burgess. To that end a detailed statement on my own career would be useful.

'. . . I explained . . . as best I could. In doing so I gave White a piece of gratuitous information, a slip which I regretted bitterly at the time . . . This information related to a trip which I had made to Franco Spain before *The Times* sent me as their accredited correspondent. It seemed that MI5 had no record of that trip, and had assumed that *The Times* had sent me to Spain direct from a desk in Fleet Street.

'White did not take long to ask me if I had paid for the

*Sir Dick Goldsmith White, then head of MI5.

first journey out of my own resources. It was a nasty little question because the enterprise had been suggested to me and financed by the Soviet Secret Service . . . and a glance at my bank balance for the period would have shown that I had no means for gallivanting around Spain.'

Such slips can be fatal for the man being interrogated. Philby described how he was questioned several times in the following weeks. What is fascinating is his account of the interrogation of John Skardon, one of the most deadly and skilled questioners in MI5. Says Philby: 'he was scrupulously courteous, his manner verging on the exquisite; nothing could have been more flattering than the cosy warmth of his interest in my views and actions. . . . During our first long conversation I detected and evaded two little traps which he laid for me with deftness and precision . . . on my finances . . . I took the opportunity of giving him some harmless misinformation. My object in doing so was a serious one. I had been able to invent plausible explanations for most of the oddities of my career, but not all of them. Where my invention failed, I could only plead lapses of memory. I just could not remember this person or that incident. The probing of my finances gave me a chance of confirming the erratic working of my memory.'

One of the most efficient interrogating teams ever established was that of the 'London Cage', known for short as KPM, set up at 6-7 Kensington Palace Gardens, London, at the end of World War II. A special intelligence unit of German-speaking interrogators was given the task of questioning German prisoners-of-war.

If ever there is the absolutely right psychological moment for interrogation it is at the end of a war when the victor can question the vanquished. The latter are not merely defeated, but bewildered: they know their own world has been brought down in ruins and that co-operation with their former enemy is perhaps the best if not the only way of being quickly released from imprisonment.

There is also one bribe the victors can hold out to them: the promise of locating their families.

The aim of the interrogators in this case was to separate the war criminals from the rest, to find out who were the real villains and who were simply honest soldiers carrying out orders. There was also a careful scrutiny of any spies who might have been infiltrated into the ranks of prisoners-of-war and to check disturbing reports (later proved to be unfounded) that the Nazis had gone underground after their defeat and were planning a clandestine organisation.

Among those chosen for interrogators were barristers (used to cross-examination), former journalists who knew Germany and some who had themselves been prisoners-of-war in Germany. The last named had the advantage of being fully aware of German questioning techniques.

The head of this team was Lieut-Col. Alexander Paterson Scotland, who had actually served in the German Army for a short while. In his early years he had been cattle-farming in South-West Africa, then under German control, and when there was a native rising and the Germans appealed for recruits to join their Forces, Scotland had taken a temporary commission in the German Army. On the strength of his fluent German and his knowledge of German military organisation Lieut-Col. Scotland became an Intelligence Officer in both world wars and was one of the most formidable interrogators of all time.

The fact that he had served in the German Army many years previously was carefully disguised. Instead the legend was built up that he had infiltrated the German General

The London Cage: as it is today

Staff in World War II and knew all that had been going on.

It was a bluff which worked remarkably well and caused many senior German officers to tell the British a great deal of secret information.

'Toni' believes that the Chinese have today brought interrogation and brain-washing to a fine art without ever descending to physical torture.

'One of my jobs was to interview people who had been imprisoned by the Chinese,' he told me. 'We had come across cases of brain-washing among prisoners-of-war in Korea, and we suspected that the Chinese might have similar methods.

'Some of those imprisoned had been agents, yet I discovered that not a single one of them had been tortured or illtreated in a physical sense. What was interesting about

A Vietcong suspect being interrogated by S. Vietmanese soldiers

these interviews was that they revealed that considerable brain-washing had been carried out without the prisoners being aware of it. It was all much subtler than some of the so-called "confessions" which the Russians obtain by cruder brainwashing.

'One agent of ours who came back from Shanghai seemed to be more hostile to his own country, because he claimed the USA had done nothing to get him released, than towards the Chinese who had arrested him.

'He insisted he had not been badly treated, though admitted he had been kept in solitary confinement for several days without being allowed any exercise or having been questioned.

'But when the Chinese did question him they relaxed controls. He was allowed to exercise in a courtyard each day, he was given better food, books and writing material.

'The Chinese would hint that the CIA did not seem concerned about his fate. I am certain that he talked a great deal to the Chinese and gave them information he should have kept to himself. But where the Chinese were clever is that they did not ask him obvious questions about his work, or what he was doing in China. They encouraged him to talk on generalities – computers, aeronautics and technical matters – often luring him into indiscretions by the most innocent of questions.

'I am sure he was given a truth-drug, probably in his food, but we never did discover what it was. My own guess is that he was given marijuana in his food. Later I learned he had become a pot addict. I am afraid we never gave him any more work.'

Very cunningly the Chinese decorated his cell with paper streamers and gave him a farewell banquet the night before he left prison!

Chapter 12

The reason why

Espionage is perhaps unhappily more necessary today than ever it was in the past. Of course it has changed considerably in the past twenty years and will continue to develop new forms and methods. The advent of nuclear weapons has forced all the great powers possessing them to keep a constant watch on one another.

The most revolutionary tactic that the advent of nuclear weapons has brought about is 'instant espionage'. This is the kind of espionage that is collected all the time by spy planes with electronic eyes, by satellites recording every detail their cameras can pick up and by a host of other electronic gadgets passing on information to a central computer system which will within seconds analyse and transmit the data to Intelligence headquarters.

In this computer-controlled war of the two great spy services of the world, the United States and the Soviet Union, something like an electronic stalemate has been achieved. This moment of truth was recognised when the USA and the Soviet Union achieved a tacit understanding over the case of the RB-47 fliers.

Manned by a crew of six, a USAF RB-47 reconnaissance plane on an 'electromagnetic research' mission was shot down by a soviet fighter over the Barents Sea. The Russians imprisoned the crew in Lubianka jail, usually kept for spy prisoners. Meanwhile in the USA two Russian agents named Melekh and Hirsch were arrested by the FBI. In Melekh's possession was found details of the US space programme and a Spacecraft guide, while Hirsch had on him a scrap of paper which asked him to get information on:

'Description of long range multiple throwing A/S weapon, the MK 31;
'Hydro-acoustic devices, the QCB type;
'Radio-hydro-acoustic buoys;
'Manual "Compar Pac ASW Hunter".'

The Bell System Telstar Satellite

One of the American RB-47 fliers reported missing

Lubyanka prison

**Yuri Vladimirovich
Andropov**

Richard Helms

This is the kind of high-powered technical information which the modern espionage service is out to get. And although each side denied having put pressure on the other, and each insisted that the Melekh and Hirsch and the RB-47 cases had no connection, the air crew were set free and the two Russian agents allowed to go home without charges being brought.

Similarly in the fight for supremacy in probes into outer space and the race for getting the first man on the moon, again, though neither will admit it, the real driving force behind both the USA and Soviet Russia has been the need for intelligence.

The technical know-how acquired from putting rockets and satellites into outer space enables both powers to step up their spies-in-the sky operations. These were those who at one time believed that the first power to put a man on the moon would be able to dominate the world by establishing spotting stations there, or setting up remote-control nuclear bomb launching pads.

While the USA has spent a fortune on sending men to the moon, the Soviet Union has also disbursed vast sums on earth-controlled mechanical and electronic probes both of the moon and distant planets. Each side will try as far as possible to monitor and spy on the space explorations of the other: each will try to keep the other guessing as to the real reasons for such operations.

The constant watch kept on each other's space probes has greatly added to the cost of espionage for America and Russia. Meanwhile what are lesser powers doing? The British have kept their Secret Service budget down recently. It was the view of Mr Harold Macmillan, when he was British Prime Minister in the late 'fifties and early 'sixties, that sixty per cent of intelligence work was a waste of time.

This is true up to a point, but often what may seem unimportant at the time becomes vital later on. Without following up a great deal of trivia and routine, unpromising inquiries, an Intelligence Service may suffer severely.

In one respect the British are curiously stubborn. Over the past two centuries they have refused to name the head of their Secret Service, even making it an offence under the Official Secrets Act for it to be revealed. Yet in almost every other nation the Secret Service chief is a well known figure like Yuri Andropov, of the KGB, or Richard Helms, of the CIA.

Perhaps the British will eventually change this policy because not only is the identity of the current head of their Secret Service known to most foreign Intelligence Services, but twice in recent years both his identity and that of his predecessor have been revealed in the foreign press. In February, 1973, the Hamburg magazine *Stern* stated that he was Sir John Rennie, a Deputy Under-Secretary of State at the Foreign Office, while reporting that his son and daughter-in-law had been sent for trial, accused of possessing Chinese heroin. Until then British newspaper reports of the hearings of this case had not revealed the names of the defendants, because the identity of the father was covered by what is known as a D-notice, which forbids publication of anything that might harm the country's security.

The prolonged armed confrontation between Israel and the Arab countries has resulted in both sides stepping up their espionage activities and Israel, a small nation barely 25 years old, has developed one of the most efficient Secret Services of any small power. Indeed it has been the smaller nations who in the last few years have posed a new menace for the major spy services of the world – the technique of hi-jacking planes usually for the purpose of demanding the release of political prisoners or spies. These hi-jackings have taken place more often than not in such countries as Germany, Switzerland, USA and Italy, thus giving extra work for the counter-espionage services in those territories. Most of these hi-jackings have been carried out by bands of guerrilla spies, employed, not by governments, but by unofficial secret services or guerrilla organisations like those of some Latin American countries and the various Arab Liberation groups sworn to wage a war of nerves on Israel.

Sir John Rennie

Keeping a watch for the hi-jackers with political aims has kept the counter-espionage services of all the great powers on their toes. They have suddenly learned that it is not only in fiction that a small group of desperadoes can hold a powerful nation to ransom. To fight a band of fanatics who hold their lives cheaply is never easy. Above all there is the constant fear that one day such a group will obtain possession of a nuclear weapon and, in making their demands, will pose the threat of the destruction of a whole city.

Another new development is the war of ideas and in this respect the spreading of false information has become almost as important as spying. This is now carried out as a political weapon to mask the real intentions of the power using it. The Russians actually have a Department of Disinformation in their Secret Service. Another of their less likeable tactics is the planting of false manuscripts, or *samizdats*, as they are known, in the Western World.

Are the letters on the following pages written by the same person? Or could they be forged?

Dear Sir,

Я не знаю, если можно
перевести с Полугин и если
Вам понравится.

2 месяца тому назад я
прислал и перевод на
английский яз. JOSEPH
другую мою репортаж (25 стр)
из Синкианга и Северного
Тибета (как кажется я
действую хорошо в моем профессе
будущих совенко-китайских
отношений. В репортаже
важное место посвещено тре-
нировке северотибетских
гериллас (на Западе знают
только джамба) лагер-
ный жизни племени - воину
Вьену в 1966 успешно чудалось

tento druhý argument jasně
dokazuje zrůdnou zkázu socia-
listického mravního kodexu
a nabytí hnusující rysů
imperialistické zvlčilosti,
nerku-li zhovadilosti.

Pro vás míru a vlasti zdar
pro ně zdar v diamantech
rajkách
a uveřejněných objevech

Váš
Vládce Malajska
alias Tygr Tořešovy úžiny
(AMAZON)

všechny moře (K celkem
prodány Praha i Kanada
(AFERER ROCOB)
K 20% ziskem !!! a vše do
haléře investovat do akce
N. guinea. Reparuji K
příští zdařné akci. URČITĚ
ZAČÁTEK !!!!

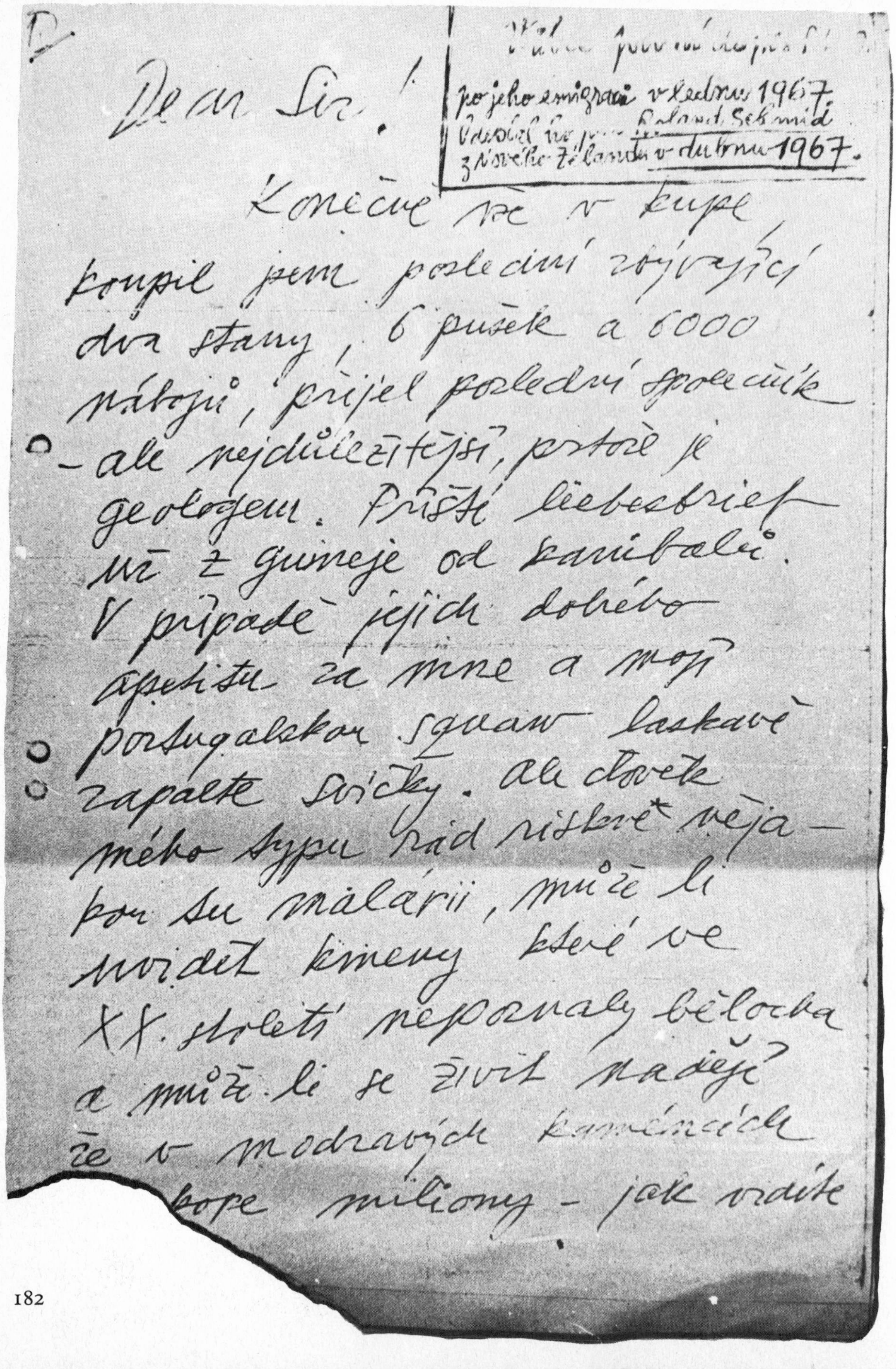

Vůbec první dopis !?
po jeho emigraci v lednu 1967.
Odeslal ho pan Roland Schmid
z Nového Zélandu v dubnu 1967.

Dear Sir !

Konečně vše v kupě
koupil jsem poslední zbývající
dva stany, 6 pušek a 6000
nábojů, přijel poslední společník
– ale nejdůležitější, protože je
geologem. Příště liebesbrief
už z guineje od kanibalů.
V případě jejich dobrého
apetitu za mne a moji
portugalskou squaw laskavě
zapalte svíčky. Ale člověk
mého typu rád riskne* veja-
kou tu malárii, může li
uvidět kmeny které ve
XX. století nepoznaly běločka
a může li se živit nadějí
že v modravých kamenech
kope miliony – jak vidíte

D/

Dear Sir !

... poslal mi dopis !
po jeho emigraci v lednu 1967
... Roland Schmid
z Nového Zélandu v dubnu 1967.

Konečně se v kupě
koupil jsem poslední zbývající
dva stany, 6 pušek a 6000
nábojů, přijel poslední společník
– ale nejdůležitější, protože je
geologem. Příště liebesbrief
už z Guineje od kanibalů.
V případě jejich dobrého
apetitu za mne a moji
portugalskou squaw laskavě
zapalte svíčky. Ale člověk
mého typu rád riskuje věja-
por su malárii, může li
vidět kmeny které ve
XX. století nepoznaly bělocha
a může li se živit nadějí
že v modravých kamíncích
kope miliony – jak vidíte

tento druhý argument jasně
dokazuje zrůdnou zkázu socia-
listického mravního kodexu
a nabytí hnusných rysů
imperialistické nevčělosti,
nerku-li zhovadilosti.

Pro vás míru a vlasti zdar
pro mě zdar v diamantech
rajkách
a unešeních objevech

Váš
Vládce Malajska
alias Tygr Torésovy úžiny
(AMAZAN)

všechny volí KČ celkem
podány Wallick t Canady
(různě 2008)
k 20% ziskem !!! a vše do
haléře investovat do akce
N.Guinea. Revanšuji se t
příště zdárné akci. DRŽTE
PALCE !!!

эмиграция в Казахстан.
(могу прислать различных
фотоснимков).

— Эти тоже (фото) репортажа
жа з Казахско-китайской границы
летом 66 г. (Только 3 фото).

Как говорит Илья Эренбург —
"...если пригодится "об ней",
если нет, бросте в "дально-
сти".

О Бамберг сейчас писать
не рад — я на долгий ящик
отложу. Сам признаюсь
я Лондоне.

Сердечно Ваш

ANALYTICAL & CONSULTING CHEMISTS
UNION INTERNATIONALE DES
LABORATOIRES INDÉPENDANTS

YOUR REF.   3rd December 1971

Dear Sirs,

        As requested by your letter of the 30th November, I
have compared the handwriting on the following:

Questioned
        Photocopy (2 sheets) of letter commencing "Dear Sir!
Konecne ..."   Mostly written Czech (?)

Authentic
        Original of 3-page letter, being Item B referred to in our
Report of 5th November 1971.

        In such cases it is my practice to select, if possible, at
least 10 diagnostic characteristics of the authentic writing, and
to compare each in turn with the same characteristics of the
questioned writing, giving marks out of 10 according to their
importance and degree of similarity.

        In the present instance the material at my disposal
enabled me to select only 9 such points likely to give dependable
information.   On applying the above procedure I arrive at a total
marking of approximately 65.

        The above results mean that there is a strong probability
that the two documents show the normal handwriting of the same
person.

        It is not possible to be more certain because of the language
differences and the fact that the authentic writing is on a photocopy.
However, the reverse conclusion seems very unlikely.

                        Yours faithfully,

P.S. The book and 3 documents are returned herewith.

This has been so cleverly done on a number of occasions that the exact purpose behind the ploy has not even been detected. There are other instances though, where such blatant use has been made of *samizdats* that the reason behind them is obvious. If there is a dissident writer in Russia who, though claiming to be a good Communist, is critical of the regime, a member of the KGB will concoct a manuscript, partly genuinely written by the man in question, but into which is interpolated in skilfully disguised handwriting violent attacks on the Soviet Government and on communism as a creed.

This will be smuggled out of Russia, given to an intermediary who poses as a friend of the writer and promptly sells it to a Western newspaper or magazine. When it is published, the KGB use this as an excuse to arrest the writer on charges of treason to the state.

Finally, a note of warning to those who may take too seriously the Macmillan theory that 'sixty per cent of espionage is a waste of time'. It is perfectly true that espionage costs, like any other budget costs, must be scrutinised and challenged when they do not produce results.

But effective espionage means constant vigilance. And vigilance costs money. Yet cheese-paring economies in not being vigilant can cost a great deal more in the long run.

There is the case of Anatoli Yakovlev, wartime Soviet Vice-Consul in New York. Then Russia was an ally of the USA. Perhaps it seemed a waste of time and money to watch Yakovlev. Yet if Yakovlev had been consistently shadowed, Dr Klaus Fuchs would have been caught before he could do much damage, and so would Harry Gold, Julius Rosen and other traitors. This precaution would have cost thousands of dollars, but it would have saved atomic secrets worth many millions.

From Yakovlev's organisation the Russians got information which advanced their atom bomb programme by at least eighteen months, not to mention radar secrets and plans for the H-bomb and guided missiles. It was through Yakovlev that the Russians contacted five left-wing scientists working in the Radiation Laboratory and organised them into a Communist cell.

The easiest way to check such plots is by keeping watch on all Russian diplomats. Sooner or later they will lead the way to the undercover agent who does the really deadly work.

I should also like to strike a light note, but with an underlying serious moral, to end up with. No doubt there are many mad, bizarre and utterly unpractical ideas submitted each year by spy-masters and spies. Mostly they can be written off, but sometimes they succeed when all else fails.

In World War II General 'Wild Bill' Donovan employed a 'think tank' that came up with some of the craziest ideas.

Hitler and Hess

One such was a plan to drive Hitler insane by exposing him to pornography. This project was worked out by some of Donovan's psycho-analysts who had obtained reports on psychological examinations of the Fuhrer and decided on the strength of these that he could be undermined with vast quantities of salacious literature.

A collection of all the obscenest German books the OSS researchers could find was assembled with the object of putting them on a plane and dropping them in the vicinity of Hitler's HQ. But the colonel in charge of this flight mission finally vetoed it as being 'the craziest scheme I have ever heard'.

Not less crazy in its initial stages was the British plan to stage real sabotage operations against *British* factories in World War II with *enemy* sabotage equipment. In case you may think this last sentence is a printer's error, or an author's mental blackout, this is how it was done. Two British agents, code-named 'Mutt' and 'Jeff', had posed as double-agents and won the Germans' confidence. British Secret Service planners decided to lure the Germans into parachuting sabotage material into Britain by getting 'Mutt' and 'Jeff' to promise to blow up a generating plant at Bury St Edmunds. The Germans fell for this and in February, 1943, parachuted in a new transmitter and £200 to 'Mutt' and 'Jeff'. This was followed by a further £800, another radio set and sabotage equipment in two further drops.

An explosion was staged at the generating plant, not in effect doing much damage, but sufficiently deceiving the Germans that their propaganda department later claimed that more than 150 people had been killed. Thus in one action the Germans were robbed of money and sabotage equipment, enabling the British to find out how they carried out sabotage and at the same time their own spy network was successfully infiltrated.

Even astrology has been effectively used in espionage down the ages. John Dee, Queen Elizabeth I's astrologer, was one of the ablest spies of his day and not only used astrology to bamboozle visiting potentates and rival agents, but camouflaged many of his secret messages under astrological symbols. But in World War II astrology took on a new significance among the Allied powers because it was well known that many of the leading Nazis were fanatical devotees of the art.

Hitler's astrology chart

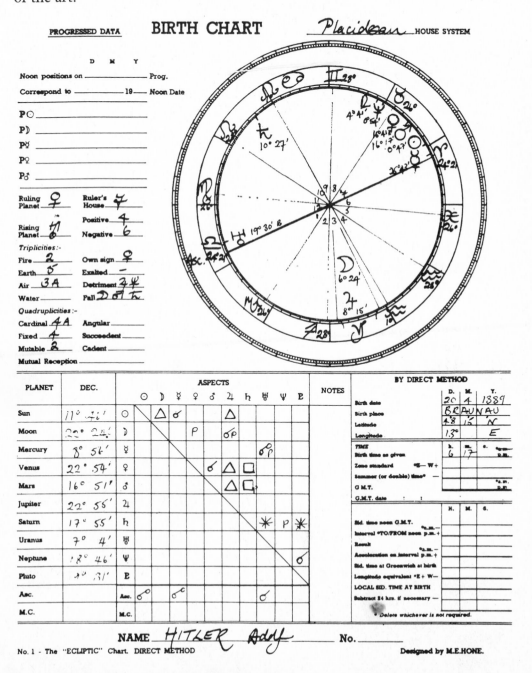

**The plane in which Rudolf
Hess landed in Britain**

Both sides used astrology in the war of nerves. The Germans sent over to America, before the latter's entry into the war, a number of astrologers who forecast German victories and the downfall of the Allies. This was fine while they were winning as all the General Staff had to do was to tip off their tame astrologers in advance of each successful coup. These horoscopes were published in many US newspapers and magazines. To counteract this the British actually engaged astrologers in the Intelligence Service, not only to get pro-Ally forecasts published, but to get them to analyse Nazi intentions by studying their horoscopes.

Spending money on astrologers to work out what Hitler's next move was likely to be may seem an awful waste of money and at best a speculative gamble. But it was known that both he and Rudolf Hess consulted certain astrologers before making decisions. One British agent was Louis de Wohl, a Hungarian astrologer, whose job was to forecast Hitler's intuitions and what he was likely to do. He had learned the methods of Karl Klafft, Hitler's favourite astrologer, and was therefore able to work out similar horoscopes on Hitler.

One of Ian Fleming's wilder ideas even before he became Deputy of the Director of Naval Intelligence was to plant some fake horoscopes of Hess to lure him to Britain in the hope of bringing off a negotiated peace. There is still some doubt as to actually what happened. But clearly somebody took up Fleming's idea and an astrologer was persuaded to advise Hess to fly secretly to Britain. Hess landed in Scotland after piloting a plane by himself, asked to see the Duke of Hamilton (for whom he had oviously been told to inquire), was arrested and interrogated.

If this seems a tall story, two points will perhaps lend credence to it. Ernst Schulte-Strahaus, who was Hess's astrological adviser, was arrested by the Nazis immediately after Hess's flight and the Gestapo started to round-up a number of astrologers. And Kapitan zur Alfred Wolff, Admiral Doenitz's flag officer, was insistent after the war that Hess's defection had been planned by the British Secret Service.

Which all goes to show that in the art of spying, imagination, even of the zaniest quality, can sometimes produce worthwhile ideas. There is always scope for the wildest flights of fantasy in the 'think tanks' of the spy services.

Acknowledgements:

Associated Press
Popperfoto
British Film Archives
National Portrait Gallery
The Victoria and Albert Museum
The British Museum
Reg Wilson
Camera Press
Keystone
Punch
The Imperial War Museum
The Radio Times Hulton Picture Library
The Crown
Topix
David King
United Press International
United Artists Corporation Ltd
Eon Productions
Management Investigation Services
Pinkerton's inc.
Victor Gollancz Ltd.

The illustrations in this book are drawn by:

Michael Jackson
Robin Lawrie
Peter Dennis
Ken Kirkland